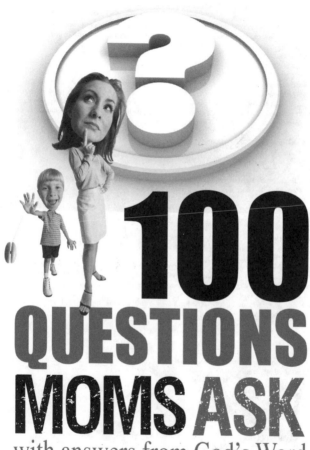

100 QUESTIONS MOMS ASK

with answers from God's Word

FAMILY
Christian Stores

Scripture quotations are taken from:

The Holy Bible, King James Version (KJV)

The Holy Bible, New International Version (NIV) Copyright © 1973, 1978, 1984, by International Bible Society. Used by permission of Zondervan Publishing House. All rights reserved.

The Holy Bible, New King James Version (NKJV) Copyright © 1982 by Thomas Nelson, Inc. Used by permission.

Holy Bible, New Living Translation, (NLT) copyright © 1996. Used by permission of Tyndale House Publishers, Inc., Wheaton, Illinois 60189. All rights reserved.

The Message (MSG)- This edition issued by contractual arrangement with NavPress, a division of The Navigators, U.S.A. Originally published by NavPress in English as THE MESSAGE: The Bible in Contemporary Language copyright 2002-2003 by Eugene Peterson. All rights reserved.

The New American Standard Bible®, (NASB) Copyright © 1960, 1962, 1963, 1968, 1971, 1972, 1973, 1975, 1977, 1995 by The Lockman Foundation. Used by permission.

New Century Version®. (NCV) Copyright © 1987, 1988, 1991 by Word Publishing, a division of Thomas Nelson, Inc. All rights reserved. Used by permission.

The Holman Christian Standard Bible™ (HCSB) Copyright © 1999, 2000, 2001 by Holman Bible Publishers. Used by permission.

Cover Design Kim Russell / Wahoo Designs

Page Layout by Bart Dawson

ISBN 978-1-58334-009-7

Printed in the United States of America

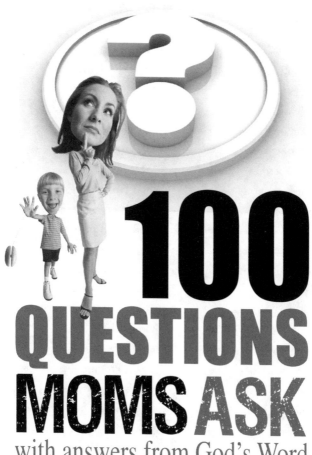

100
QUESTIONS
MOMS ASK
with answers from God's Word

INDEX OF TOPICS

Introduction

Because you're reading this book, you probably answer to the name "Mom," "Mother," "Mommy," or some variation thereof—if so, congratulations. As a loving mother, you have been blessed by your children and by God.

As a thoughtful woman living in a challenging world, you probably have questions, lots of questions. And if you've got questions, God has answers. Your challenge, of course, is to discover those answers (from God's Holy Word) and then apply them to the challenges of everyday living. And this book can help.

This text contains 100 questions that Christian mothers are likely to ask, along with answers based upon truths contained in God's ultimate guidebook: the Holy Bible.

Motherhood is both a priceless gift from God and an unrelenting responsibility. This text is intended to remind you that, when it comes to the tough job of being a responsible mother, you and God, working together, are destined to do great things for your kids and for the world.

As a busy mom, I get stressed. What can I do?

THE QUICK ANSWER

One way to battle the rigors of parenting is to slow down long enough to count your blessings, starting with your family.

Count Your Blessings

I will bless them and the places surrounding my hill.
I will send down showers in season;
there will be showers of blessings.
Ezekiel 34:26 NIV

Because you are a mother, you have been specially blessed by the Creator. God has given you blessings that are, in truth, simply too numerous to count. Your blessings include life, family, freedom, friends, talents, and possessions, for starters. But, your greatest blessing—a priceless treasure that is yours for the asking—is God's gift of salvation through Christ Jesus.

The gifts you receive from God are multiplied when you share them with others. Today, give thanks to God for your blessings and demonstrate your gratitude by sharing those blessings with your family, with your friends, and with the world.

Do we not continually pass by blessings innumerable without notice, and instead fix our eyes on what we feel to be our trials and our losses, and think and talk about these until our whole horizon is filled with them, and we almost begin to think we have no blessings at all?

Hannah Whitall Smith

When you and I are related to Jesus Christ, our strength and wisdom and peace and joy and love and hope may run out, but His life rushes in to keep us filled to the brim. We are showered with blessings, not because of anything we have or have not done, but simply because of Him.

Anne Graham Lotz

I discovered that sorrow was not to be feared but rather endured with hope and expectancy that God would use it to visit and bless my life.

Jill Briscoe

A PRAYER FOR MOMS

Lord, let me be a mother who counts her blessings, and let me be Your faithful servant as I give praise to the Giver of all things good. You have richly blessed my life, Lord. Let me, in turn, be a blessing to my family and my world—and may the glory be Yours forever. Amen

QUESTION 2

What does the Bible say about putting God first in my life?

THE QUICK ANSWER

God's Word is clear: If you put Him first in every aspect of your life, you'll be blessed. But if you relegate God to a position of lesser importance, you'll distance yourself from His blessings.

Who's First?

Do not worship any other gods besides me.
Exodus 20:3 NLT

As you think about the nature of your relationship with God, remember this: you will always have some type of relationship with Him—it is inevitable that your life must be lived in relationship to God. The question is not if you will have a relationship with Him; the burning question is whether or not that relationship will be one that seeks to honor Him.

Are you willing to place God first in your life? And, are you willing to welcome God's Son into your heart? Unless you can honestly answer these questions with a resounding yes, then your relationship with God isn't what it could be or should be. Thankfully, God is always available, He's always ready to forgive, and He's waiting to hear from you now. The rest, of course, is up to you.

Our ultimate aim in life is not to be healthy, wealthy, prosperous, or problem free. Our ultimate aim in life is to bring glory to God.

Anne Graham Lotz

When all else is gone, God is still left. Nothing changes Him.

Hannah Whitall Smith

God deserves first place in your life . . . and you deserve the experience of putting Him there.

Marie T. Freeman

A PRAYER FOR MOMS

Dear Lord, Your love is eternal and Your laws are everlasting. When I obey Your commandments, I am blessed. Today, I invite You to reign over every corner of my heart. I will have faith in You, Father. I will sense Your presence; I will accept Your love; I will trust Your will; and I will praise You for the Savior of my life: Your Son Jesus. Amen

What does the Bible say about the example that I should set for my family?

THE QUICK ANSWER

Your life is a sermon. The words you choose to speak may have some impact on others, but not nearly as much impact as the life you choose to live. God wants you to be a positive role model to your family, to your friends, and to the world.

What Kind of Example?

You should be an example to the believers in speech,
in conduct, in love, in faith, in purity.
1 Timothy 4:12 HCSB

Our children learn from the lessons we teach and the lives we live, but not necessarily in that order. As mothers, we serve as unforgettable role models for our children and grandchildren. Hopefully, the lives we lead and the choices we make will serve as enduring examples of the spiritual abundance that is available to all who worship God and obey His commandments.

What kind of example are you? Are you the kind of mother whose life serves as a genuine example of patience and righteousness? Are you a woman whose behavior serves as a positive role model for others? Are you the kind of mom whose actions, day in and day out, are based upon kindness, faithfulness, and a sincere love for the Lord? If so, you are not only blessed by God, but you are also a powerful force for good in a world that desperately needs positive influences such as yours.

Corrie ten Boom advised, "Don't worry about what you do not understand. Worry about what you do understand in the Bible but do not live by." And that's sound advice because our families and friends are watching . . . and so, for that matter, is God.

Your light is the truth of the Gospel message itself as well as your witness as to Who Jesus is and what He has done for you. Don't hide it.

Anne Graham Lotz

A PRAYER FOR MOMS

Lord, make me a worthy example to my family and friends. And, let my words and my deeds serve as a testimony to the changes You have made in my life. Let me praise You, Father, by following in the footsteps of Your Son, and let others see Him through me. Amen

What does the Bible say about God's plans for my family and for me?

THE QUICK ANSWER

God has a wonderful plan for you and your loved ones. And the time to start looking for that plan—and living it—is now. Discovering God's plan begins with prayer, but it doesn't end there. You've also got to work at it.

Very Big Plans

Teach me to do Your will, for You are my God.
May Your gracious Spirit lead me on level ground.
Psalm 143:10 HCSB

The Bible makes it clear: God has plans—very big plans—for you and your family. But He won't force His plans upon you—if you wish to experience the abundance that God has in store, you must be willing to accept His will and follow His Son.

As Christians, you and your family members should ask yourselves this question: "How closely can we make our plans match God's plans?" The more closely you manage to follow the path that God intends for your lives, the better.

Do you and your loved ones have questions or concerns about the future? Take them to God in prayer. Do you have hopes and expectations? Talk to God about your dreams. Are you and your family members carefully planning for the days and weeks ahead? Consult God as you establish your priorities. Turn every concern over to your Heavenly Father, and sincerely seek His guidance—prayerfully, earnestly, and often. Then, listen for His answers . . . and trust the answers that He gives.

God prepared a plan for your life alone—and neither man nor the devil can destroy that plan.

Kay Arthur

We will stand amazed to see the topside of the tapestry and how God beautifully embroidered each circumstance into a pattern for our good and His glory.

Joni Eareckson Tada

A PRAYER FOR MOMS

Lord, You have a plan for my life that is grander than I can imagine. Let Your purposes be my purposes. Let Your will be my will. When I am confused, give me clarity. When I am frightened, give me courage. Let me be Your faithful servant, always seeking Your guidance for my life. And, let me always be a shining beacon for Your Son today and every day that I live. Amen

QUESTION 5

I learned the Golden Rule as a child, but now that I'm an adult, what should it mean to me?

THE QUICK ANSWER

The Golden Rule applies to all believers of all ages, including you. That means that you must strive to treat other people—all people—in the same way you want to be treated. No exceptions.

A Rule That's Golden

Just as you want others to do for you, do the same for them.
Luke 6:31 HCSB

The words of Matthew 7:12 remind us that, as believers in Christ, we are commanded to treat others as we wish to be treated. This commandment is, indeed, the Golden Rule for Christians of every generation. When we weave the thread of kindness into the very fabric of our lives, we give glory to the One who gave His life for ours.

Because we are imperfect human beings, we are, on occasion, selfish, thoughtless, or cruel. But God commands us to behave otherwise. He teaches us to rise above our own imperfections and to treat others with unselfishness and love.

When we observe God's Golden Rule, we help build His kingdom here on earth. And, when we share the love of Christ, we share a priceless gift; may we share it today and every day that we live.

I have discovered that when I please Christ, I end up inadvertently serving others far more effectively.

Beth Moore

The Golden Rule starts at home, but it should never stop there.

Marie T. Freeman

It is one of the most beautiful compensations of life that no one can sincerely try to help another without helping herself.

Barbara Johnson

The #1 rule of friendship is the Golden one.

Jim Gallery

A PRAYER FOR MOMS

Lord, in all aspects of my life, let me treat others as I wish to be treated. The Golden Rule is Your rule, Father; let me make it mine. Amen

As a parent, I know how easy it is for grownups and children alike to take the wrong path. What does the Bible say about the way we should behave ourselves?

THE QUICK ANSWER

The best way to guard your steps is by walking with Jesus every day of your life. When you do, you'll be blessed, not just for a day, but for all eternity.

Following the Right Path

So don't get tired of doing what is good.
Don't get discouraged and give up, for we will reap
a harvest of blessing at the appropriate time.
Galatians 6:9 NLT

Oswald Chambers, the author of the Christian classic, *My Utmost For His Highest,* advised, "Never support an experience which does not have God as its source, and faith in God as its result." These words serve as a powerful reminder that, as Christians, we are called to walk with God and obey His commandments. But, we live in a world that presents countless temptations for adults and even more temptations for our children.

We Christians, when confronted with sin, have clear instructions: walk—or better yet run—in the opposite direction. When we do, we reap the blessings that God has promised to all those who live according to His will and His Word.

———————

Although God causes all things to work together for good for His children, He still holds us accountable for our behavior.

Kay Arthur

Either God's Word keeps you from sin, or sin keeps you from God's Word.

Corrie ten Boom

We have a decision to make—to turn away from sin or to be miserable and suffer the consequences of continual disobedience.

Vonette Bright

A PRAYER FOR MOMS

Lord, there is a right way and a wrong way to live. Let me live according to Your rules, not the world's rules. Your path is right for me, God; let me follow it every day of my life. Amen

What does the Bible say about love?

THE QUICK ANSWER

God is love, and He expects us to share His love.

Love According to God

Now these three remain: faith, hope, and love.
But the greatest of these is love.
1 Corinthians 13:13 HCSB

Love, like everything else in this wonderful world, begins and ends with God, but the middle part belongs to us. During the brief time that we have here on earth, God has given each of us the opportunity to become a loving person—or not. God has given each of us the opportunity to be kind, to be courteous, to be cooperative, and to be forgiving—or not. God has given each of us the chance to obey the Golden Rule, or to make up our own rules as we go. If we obey God's rules, we're safe, but if we do otherwise, we're headed for trouble and fast.

Here in the real world, the choices that we make have consequences. The decisions that we make and the results of those decisions determine the quality of our relationships. It's as simple as that.

Those who abandon ship the first time it enters a storm miss the calm beyond. And the rougher the storms weathered together, the deeper and stronger real love grows.

Ruth Bell Graham

It is when we come to the Lord in our nothingness, our powerlessness and our helplessness that He then enables us to love in a way which, without Him, would be absolutely impossible.

Elisabeth Elliot

Love is extravagant in the price it is willing to pay, the time it is willing to give, the hardships it is willing to endure, and the strength it is willing to spend. Love never thinks in terms of "how little," but always in terms of "how much." Love gives, love knows, and love lasts.

Joni Eareckson Tada

A PRAYER FOR MOMS

Dear Lord, today and every day, I will tell my family that I love them. And I will show my family that I love them. Amen

Sometimes it seems like the media is attacking my family. What should I do?

THE QUICK ANSWER

The modern media is sending out messages that are dangerous to your family's physical, emotional, and spiritual health. You, as a responsible parent, must decide which messages and which images are appropriate for your child. The responsibility is yours and yours alone, not that of television executives or web page designers.

Media Messages

Set your minds on what is above, not on what is on the earth.
Colossians 3:2 HCSB

Sometimes it's hard being a woman of faith especially when the world keeps pumping out messages that are contrary to your beliefs.

Beware! The media is working around the clock in an attempt to rearrange your priorities. The media says that appearance is all-important, that thinness is all-important, and that social standing is all-important. But guess what? Those messages are untrue. The important things in life have little to do with appearances. The all-important things in life have to do with your faith, your family, and your future. Period.

Because you live in the 21st century, you are relentlessly bombarded by media messages that are contrary to your faith. Take those messages with a grain of salt—or better yet, don't take them at all.

As we have by faith said no to sin, so we should by faith say yes to God and set our minds on things above, where Christ is seated in the heavenlies.

Vonette Bright

Our fight is not against any physical enemy; it is against organizations and powers that are spiritual. We must struggle against sin all our lives, but we are assured we will win.

Corrie ten Boom

A PRAYER FOR MOMS

Lord, this world is a crazy place, and I have many opportunities to stray from Your commandments. Help me to obey You! Let me keep Christ in my heart, and let me put the devil in his place: far away from me! Amen

QUESTION 9

What does the Bible teach us about praising God?

THE QUICK ANSWER

Praise Him! One of the main reasons you and your family go to church is to praise God. But, you need not wait until Sunday rolls around to thank your Heavenly Father. Instead, you can praise Him many times each day by saying silent prayers that only He can hear.

Making Time to Praise God

Therefore, through Him let us continually offer up to God a sacrifice of praise, that is, the fruit of our lips that confess His name.
Hebrews 13:15 HCSB

God has given you treasures that are beyond measure. He sent His only begotten Son to die for you, and He gave you a family to care for and to love. God has given you another day of life, and He has filled it to the brim with opportunities to celebrate and to serve. What should you do in return for God's priceless gifts? You should praise Him always.

Today, as you travel to work, as you hug your child or kiss your husband, as you gaze upon a passing cloud or marvel at a glorious sunset, think of what God has done for you, for yours, and for all of us. And, every time you notice a gift from the Giver of all things good, praise Him. His works are marvelous, His gifts are beyond understanding, and His love endures forever.

Two wings are necessary to lift our souls toward God: prayer and praise. Prayer asks. Praise accepts the answer.

Mrs. Charles E. Cowman

Nothing we do is more powerful or more life-changing than praising God.

Stormie Omartian

When we come before the Lord with praise, humbly repent of our transgressions, and in obedience present our petitions to God according to the guidelines set out for us in Scripture, He will answer.

Shirley Dobson

A PRAYER FOR MOMS

Dear Lord, today and every day I will praise You. I will come to You with hope in my heart and words of gratitude on my lips. Let my thoughts, my prayers, my words, and my deeds praise You now and forever. Amen

QUESTION 10

What does the Bible say about my daily devotional?

THE QUICK ANSWER

Time and again, the Bible stresses the need to study God's Word every day, with no exceptions. If you make your morning devotional an ironclad habit, you'll be blessed.

Every Day with God

Stay clear of silly stories that get dressed up as religion.
Exercise daily in God—no spiritual flabbiness, please!
1 Timothy 4:7 MSG

Each new day is a gift from God, and wise moms spend a few quiet moments each morning thanking the Giver. Daily life is woven together with the threads of habit, and no habit is more important to our spiritual health than the discipline of daily prayer and devotion to the Creator.

When we begin each day with heads bowed and hearts lifted, we remind ourselves of God's love, His protection, and His commandments. And if we are wise, we align our priorities for the coming day with the teachings and commandments that God has given us through His Holy Word.

Are you seeking to change some aspect of your life? Then take time out of your hectic schedule to spend time each day with your Creator. Do you seek to improve the condition of your spiritual or physical health? If so, ask for God's help and ask for it many times each day . . . starting with your morning devotional.

God is a place of safety you can run to, but it helps if you are running to Him on a daily basis so that you are in familiar territory.

Stormie Omartian

If you, too, will learn to wait upon God, to get alone with Him, and remain silent so that you can hear His voice when He is ready to speak to you, what a difference it will make in your life!

Kay Arthur

A PRAYER FOR MOMS

Lord, help me to hear Your direction for my life in the quiet moments when I study Your Holy Word. And as I go about my daily activities, let everything that I say and do be pleasing to You. Amen

What does the Bible say about prayer?

THE QUICK ANSWER

Pray early and often: One way to make sure that your heart is in tune with God is to pray often. The more you talk to the Father, the more He will talk to you.

Too Busy to Pray?

If my people who are called by my name, will humble themselves and pray and seek my face and turn from their wicked ways, then will I hear from heaven and will forgive their sin and will heal their land.

2 Chronicles 7:14 NIV

Does your family pray together often, or just at church? Are you a little band of prayer warriors, or have you retreated from God's battlefield? Do you and yours pray only at mealtimes, or do you pray much more often than that? The answer to these questions will determine, to a surprising extent, the level of your family's spiritual health.

Jesus made it clear to His disciples: they should pray always. And so should you. Genuine, heartfelt prayer changes things and it changes you. When you lift your heart to the Father, you open yourself to a never-ending source of divine wisdom and infinite love.

Your family's prayers are powerful. So, as you go about your daily activities, remember God's instructions: "Rejoice always! Pray constantly. Give thanks in everything, for this is God's will for you in Christ Jesus" (1 Thessalonians 5:16-18 HCSB). Start praying in the morning and keep praying until you fall off to sleep at night. And rest assured: God is always listening, and He always wants to hear from you and your family.

When there is a matter that requires definite prayer, pray until you believe God and until you can thank Him for His answer.

Hannah Whitall Smith

When you ask God to do something, don't ask timidly; put your whole heart into it.

Marie T. Freeman

A PRAYER FOR MOMS

Lord, make me a prayerful Christian. In good times and in bad times, in whatever state I find myself, let me turn my prayers to You. You always hear my prayers, God; let me always pray them! Amen

Sometimes my life doesn't seem very exciting. Why should I be excited about life?

THE QUICK ANSWER

Today is a cause for celebration! Psalm 118:24 has clear instructions for the coming day: "This is the day which the LORD has made; let us rejoice and be glad in it." Plan your day—and your life—accordingly.

Celebrate!

Celebrate God all day, every day. I mean, revel in him!
Philippians 4:4 MSG

Are you a mom who celebrates life? Hopefully you are! God has richly blessed you, and He wants you to rejoice in His gifts.

God fills each day to the brim with possibilities, and He challenges each of us to use our gifts for the glory of His kingdom. When we honor the Father and place Him at the center of our lives, every day becomes a cause for celebration.

Today is a non-renewable resource—once it's gone, it's gone forever. Our responsibility—both as mothers and as believers—is to use this day in the service of God's will and in the service of

His people. When we do so, we enrich our own lives and the lives of those whom we love. And the Father smiles.

Our sense of joy, satisfaction, and fulfillment in life increases, no matter what the circumstances, if we are in the center of God's will.

Billy Graham

If you can forgive the person you were, accept the person you are, and believe in the person you will become, you are headed for joy. So celebrate your life.

Barbara Johnson

Unparalleled joy and victory come from allowing Christ to do "the hard thing" with us.

Beth Moore

A PRAYER FOR MOMS

Dear Lord, today, I will join in the celebration of life. I will be a joyful Christian, and I will share my joy with all those who cross my path. You have given me countless blessings, Lord, and today I will thank You by celebrating my life, my faith, and my Savior. Amen

This world can be a crazy place for grownups and kids alike. What should I do about the evils that I encounter? And what about the temptations my children will encounter?

THE QUICK ANSWER

Of course there is darkness in this world, but God's light can overpower any darkness. So make sure that your family's life—and faith—is built on the firm foundation of God's Word. Make sure that your children have plenty of "advance warning" (from you) about the dangers they will encounter. And keep praying that everyone in your clan will have the wisdom and the strength to avoid the darkness.

You'd Better Beware

The Lord is pleased with a good person,
but he will punish anyone who plans evil.
Proverbs 12:2 NCV

This world is God's creation, and it contains the wonderful fruits of His handiwork. But, it also contains countless opportunities to stray from God's will. Temptations are everywhere, and the devil, it seems, never takes a day off. Our task, as caring mothers, is to do all that we can to protect our families from the evils of the world.

We must recognize evil and fight it. When we observe life objectively, and when we do so with eyes and hearts that are attuned to God's Holy Word, we can no longer be neutral believers. And when we are no longer neutral, God rejoices while the devil despairs.

———————————

We are in a continual battle with the spiritual forces of evil, but we will triumph when we yield to God's leading and call on His powerful presence in prayer.

Shirley Dobson

Light is stronger than darkness—darkness cannot "comprehend" or "overcome" it.

Anne Graham Lotz

Where God's ministers are most successful, there the powers of darkness marshal their forces for the conflict.

Lottie Moon

A PRAYER FOR MOMS

Lord, strengthen my walk with You. Evil comes in many disguises, and sometimes it is only with Your help that I can recognize right from wrong. Your presence in my life enables me to choose truth and to live a life pleasing to You. May I always live in Your presence. Amen

I'm a very busy mom, without a minute to spare. Should I still try to carve out time every day for Bible study?

THE QUICK ANSWER

No matter how busy you are, you should still study your Bible every day. The Bible is unlike any other book because it is the revealed Word of God. You need to read it—carefully and prayerfully—every day.

Studying the Word

For I am not ashamed of the gospel, because it is God's power for salvation to everyone who believes.
Romans 1:16 HCSB

God's Word is unlike any other book. The Bible is a roadmap for life here on earth and for life eternal. As Christians, we are called upon to study God's Holy Word, to trust His Word, to follow its commandments, and to share its Good News with the world.

The words of Matthew 4:4 remind us that, "Man shall not live by bread alone but by every word that proceedeth out of the mouth of God" (KJV). As believers, we must study the Bible and meditate upon its meaning for our lives. Otherwise, we deprive ourselves of a priceless gift from our Creator.

Warren Wiersbe observed, "When the child of God looks into the Word of God, he sees the Son of God. And, he is transformed by the Spirit of God to share in the glory of God." God's Holy Word is, indeed, a transforming, life-changing, one-of-a-kind treasure. And, a passing acquaintance with the Good Book is insufficient for Christians who seek to obey God's Word and to understand His will. After all, men—and moms—do not live by bread alone . . .

The Reference Point for the Christian is the Bible. All values, judgments, and attitudes must be gauged in relationship to this Reference Point.

Ruth Bell Graham

Study the Bible and observe how the persons behaved and how God dealt with them. There is explicit teaching on every condition of life.

Corrie ten Boom

A PRAYER FOR MOMS

Dear Lord, the Bible is Your gift to me. Let me use it, let me trust it, and let me obey it, today and every day that I live. Amen

QUESTION 15

What does the Bible say about family life?

THE QUICK ANSWER

Your family is God's gift to you. And as a parent, you have profound responsibilities: To build your family on the firm foundation of God's love, to teach your children the wisdom of God's Word, and to serve as a positive role model to family, to friends, and to the world.

You and Your Family

Unless the Lord builds a house, its builders labor over it in vain;
unless the Lord watches over a city,
the watchman stays alert in vain.
Psalm 127:1 HCSB

As every mother knows, family life is a mixture of conversations, mediations, irritations, deliberations, commiserations, frustrations, negotiations and celebrations. In other words, the life of the typical mom is incredibly varied.

Certainly, in the life of every family, there are moments of frustration and disappointment. Lots of them. But, for those who are lucky enough to live in the presence of a close-knit, caring clan, the rewards far outweigh the frustrations.

100 QUESTIONS MOMS ASK

No family is perfect, and neither is yours. But, despite the inevitable challenges and occasional hurt feelings of family life, your clan is God's gift to you. That little band of men, women, kids, and babies is a priceless treasure on temporary loan from the Father above. Give thanks to the Giver for the gift of family . . . and act accordingly.

There is so much compassion and understanding that is gained when we've experienced God's grace firsthand within our own families.

Lisa Whelchel

One way or the other, God, who thought up the family in the first place, has the very best idea of how to bring sense to the chaos of broken relationships we see all around us. I really believe that if I remain still and listen a lot, He will share some solutions with me so I can share them with others.

Jill Briscoe

A PRAYER FOR MOMS

Lord, You have given me a family to love and to care for. Thank You, Father. I will love all the members of my family despite their imperfections. Let them love me, Dear Lord, despite mine. Amen

QUESTION 16

When it comes to my faith, I want to keep growing. How can I do that?

THE QUICK ANSWER

When it comes to your faith, God doesn't intend for you to stand still. He wants you to keep moving and growing. So promise yourself that your unfolding relationship with God will be your highest priority.

The Spiritual Journey

Grow in grace and understanding of our Master and Savior, Jesus Christ. Glory to the Master, now and forever! Yes!
2 Peter 3:18 MSG

The journey toward spiritual maturity lasts a lifetime: As Christian mothers, we can and should continue to grow in the love and the knowledge of our Savior as long as we live. When we cease to grow, either emotionally or spiritually, we do ourselves and our loved ones a profound disservice. But, if we study God's Word, if we obey His commandments, and if we live in the center of His will, we will not be "stagnant" believers; we will, instead, be growing Christians . . . and that's exactly what God wants for our lives.

Many of life's most important lessons are painful to learn. During times of heartbreak and hardship, God stands ready to protect us. As Psalm 147 promises, "He heals the brokenhearted and bandages their wounds" (NCV). In His own time and according to His master plan, God will heal us if we invite Him into our hearts.

Spiritual growth need not take place only in times of adversity. We should seek to grow in our relationship with the Lord through every season of our lives, through happy times and hard times, through times of celebration and times of pain.

In those quiet moments when we open our hearts to God, the One who made us keeps remaking us. He gives us direction, perspective, wisdom, and courage. And of course, the appropriate moment to accept those spiritual gifts is always the present one.

There is wonderful freedom and joy in coming to recognize that the fun is in the becoming.

Gloria Gaither

A PRAYER FOR MOMS

Dear Lord, the Bible tells me that You are at work in my life, continuing to help me grow and to mature in my faith. Show me Your wisdom, Father, and let me live according to Your Word and Your will. Amen

Sometimes, it's easy for me to become angry. What does the Bible say about anger?

THE QUICK ANSWER

The Bible warns us time and again that anger is only one letter away from danger. So the next time you're tempted to lose your cool, walk away before you get carried away.

Controlling Your Temper

My dear brothers and sisters, be quick to listen, slow to speak, and slow to get angry. Your anger can never make things right in God's sight.
James 1:19-20 NLT

Motherhood is vastly rewarding, but every mother knows that it can be, at times, frustrating. No family is perfect, and even the most loving mother's patience can, on occasion, wear thin.

Your temper is either your master or your servant. Either you control it, or it controls you. And the extent to which you allow anger to rule your life will determine, to a surprising degree, the quality of your relationships with others and your relationship with God.

If you've allowed anger to become a regular visitor at your house, you should pray for wisdom, for patience, and for a heart that is so filled with forgiveness that it contains no room for bitterness. God will help you terminate your tantrums if you ask Him to—and that's a good thing because anger and peace cannot coexist in the same mind.

So the next time you're tempted to lose your temper over the minor inconveniences of life, don't. Turn away from anger, hatred, bitterness, and regret. Turn instead to God. He's waiting with open arms . . . patiently.

———————————

Life is too short to spend it being angry, bored, or dull.

Barbara Johnson

Anger is the noise of the soul; the unseen irritant of the heart; the relentless invader of silence.

Max Lucado

Anger unresolved will only bring you woe.

Kay Arthur

A PRAYER FOR MOMS

Lord, when I become angry, help me to remember that You offer me peace. Let me turn to You for wisdom, for patience, and for the peace that only You can give. Amen

I want to sense God's presence. What should I do?

THE QUICK ANSWER

God isn't far away—He's right here, right now. And He's willing to talk to you right here, right now. So find a quiet place and open your heart to Him. When you do, you'll sense God's presence and His love, which, by the way, is already surrounding you and your loved ones.

He's Here

Draw near to God, and He will draw near to you.

James 4:8 HCSB

If you are a busy mother with more obligations than you have time to count, you know all too well that the demands of everyday life can, on occasion, seem overwhelming. Thankfully, even on the days when you feel overburdened, overworked, overstressed and under-appreciated, God is trying to get His message through . . . your job is to listen.

Are you tired, discouraged, or fearful? Be comforted because God is with you. Are you confused? Listen to the quiet voice of your Heavenly Father. Are you bitter? Talk with God and seek His guidance. In whatever condition you find yourself—whether you are happy or sad, victorious or vanquished, troubled or triumphant—carve out moments of silent solitude to celebrate God's gifts and to experience His presence.

The familiar words of Psalm 46:10 remind us to be still before the Creator. When we do, we encounter the awesome presence of our loving Heavenly Father, and we are comforted in the knowledge that God is not just near. He is here.

Our souls were made to live in an upper atmosphere, and we stifle and choke if we live on any lower level. Our eyes were made to look off from these heavenly heights, and our vision is distorted by any lower gazing.

Hannah Whitall Smith

God walks with us. He scoops us up in His arms or simply sits with us in silent strength until we cannot avoid the awesome recognition that yes, even now, He is here.

Gloria Gaither

A PRAYER FOR MOMS

Dear Lord, You are with me when I am strong and when I am weak. You never leave my side, even when it seems to me that You are far away. Today and every day, let me trust Your promises and let me feel Your love. Amen

When I'm worried or stressed, it's easy for me to lose perspective. What should I do?

THE QUICK ANSWER

Slow down, catch your breath, and have a chat with God. Your life is an integral part of God's grand plan. So don't be bothered by those minor inconveniences that are a part of everyday existence. Life is far too short, and besides, your children are watching and learning . . . from you.

Keeping a Proper Perspective

All I'm doing right now, friends, is showing how these things pertain to Apollos and me so that you will learn restraint and not rush into making judgments without knowing all the facts. It is important to look at things from God's point of view. I would rather not see you inflating or deflating reputations based on mere hearsay.

1 Corinthians 4:6 MSG

Even if you're the world's most thoughtful mom, you may, from time to time, lose perspective—it happens on those days when life seems out of balance and the pressures of motherhood seem overwhelming. What's needed is a fresh perspective, a restored sense of balance . . . and God.

If a temporary loss of perspective has left you worried, exhausted, or both, it's time to readjust your thought patterns. Negative thoughts are habit-forming; thankfully, so are positive ones. With practice, you can form the habit of focusing on God's priorities and your possibilities. When you do, you'll spend less time fretting about your challenges and more time praising God for His gifts.

So today and every day hereafter, pray for a sense of balance and perspective. And remember: your thoughts are intensely powerful things, so handle them with care.

Instead of being frustrated and overwhelmed by all that is going on in our world, go to the Lord and ask Him to give you His eternal perspective.

Kay Arthur

A PRAYER FOR MOMS

Dear Lord, when the pace of my life becomes frantic, slow me down and give me perspective. Give me the wisdom to realize that the problems of today are only temporary but that Your love is eternal. When I become discouraged, keep me steady and sure, so that I might do Your will here on earth and then live with You forever in heaven. Amen

QUESTION 20

What does the Bible teach us about worship?

THE QUICK ANSWER

The best way for you and your family to worship God is to worship Him sincerely and often.

Family Worship

But an hour is coming, and is now here, when the true worshipers will worship the Father in spirit and truth. Yes, the Father wants such people to worship Him. God is Spirit, and those who worship Him must worship in spirit and truth.

John 4:23-24 HCSB

When you insist that your family worship God, you are to be praised. By worshipping your Creator—and by teaching your children to do likewise—you make a powerful statement about the place that God occupies in your life.

Ours is a society in which too many parents have abandoned the moral leadership of their families, often with tragic consequences. People who neglect to worship God, either thoughtlessly or intentionally, invite untold suffering into their own lives and into the lives of their loved ones.

Every day provides opportunities to put God where He belongs: at the center of our hearts. May we worship Him, and only Him, always. And, may we encourage the members of our family to do the same.

To worship Him in truth means to worship Him honestly, without hypocrisy, standing open and transparent before Him.

Anne Graham Lotz

God asks that we worship Him with our concentrated minds as well as with our wills and emotions. A divided and scattered mind is not effective.

Catherine Marshall

In Biblical worship you do not find the repetition of a phrase; instead, you find the worshipers rehearsing the character of God and His ways, reminding Him of His faithfulness and His wonderful promises.

Kay Arthur

A PRAYER FOR MOMS

Heavenly Father, let today and every day be a time of worship for me and my family. Let us worship You, not only with words, but also with deeds. In the quiet moments of the day, let us praise You and thank You for creating us, loving us, guiding us, and saving us. Amen

What does the Bible say about God's commandments?

THE QUICK ANSWER

God's commandments are eternal and absolute. And God has given us His commandments for a reason: to obey them. These commandments are not suggestions, helpful hints, or friendly reminders—they are rules we must live by . . . or else!

His Commandments

Teach me Your way, O LORD; I will walk in Your truth.
Psalm 86:11 NASB

God gave us His commandments for a reason: so that we might obey them and be blessed. Elisabeth Elliot advised, "Obedience to God is our job. The results of that obedience are God's." These words should serve to remind us that obedience is imperative. But, we live in a world that presents us with countless temptations to disobey God's laws.

When we stray from God's path, we suffer. So, whenever we are confronted with sin, we have clear instructions: we must walk—or better yet run—in the opposite direction.

The Ten Commandments were given to evoke fear and reverence for the Holy One so that obedience and blessing might result.

Beth Moore

Don't worry about what you do not understand. Worry about what you do understand in the Bible but do not live by.

Corrie ten Boom

Only grief and disappointment can result from continued violation of the divine principles that underlie the spiritual life.

A. W. Tozer

To yield to God means to belong to God, and to belong to God means to have all His infinite power. To belong to God means to have all.

Hannah Whitall Smith

A PRAYER FOR MOMS

Thank You, Dear Lord, for loving me enough to give me rules to live by. Let me live by Your commandments, and let me lead others to do the same. Let me walk righteously in Your way, Dear Lord, this day and every day. Amen

It's a noisy world. What does the Bible say about finding time for quiet reflection?

THE QUICK ANSWER

Time and again, God's Word encourages believers to quiet themselves and spend silent moments with the Father. So begin each day with a few minutes of quiet time to organize your thoughts and praise your Creator.

Your Noisy World

Be silent before the Lord and wait expectantly for Him.
Psalm 37:7 HCSB

Face it: We live in a noisy world, a world filled with distractions, frustrations, and complications. But if we allow those distractions to separate us from God's peace, we do ourselves a profound disservice.

Are you one of those busy moms who rush through the day with scarcely a single moment for quiet contemplation and prayer? If so, it's time to reorder your priorities.

Nothing is more important than the time you spend with your Savior. So be still and claim the inner peace that is your spiritual birthright: the peace of Jesus Christ. It is offered freely;

it has been paid for in full; it is yours for the asking. So ask. And then share.

———

Jesus taught us by example to get out of the rat race and recharge our batteries.

Barbara Johnson

The manifold rewards of a serious, consistent prayer life demonstrate clearly that time with our Lord should be our first priority.

Shirley Dobson

The Lord Jesus, available to people much of the time, left them, sometimes a great while before day, to go up to the hills where He could commune in solitude with His Father.

Elisabeth Elliot

A PRAYER FOR MOMS

Lord, Your Holy Word is a light unto the world; let me study it, trust it, and share it with all who cross my path. Let me discover You, Father, in the quiet moments of the day. And, in all that I say and do, help me to be a worthy witness as I share the Good News of Your perfect Son and Your perfect Word. Amen

I've made plenty of mistakes, and I can't seem to make peace with the past. What should I do?

THE QUICK ANSWER

Everybody makes mistakes—wise people learn from them. And remember that the past is past, so don't live there. If you're focused on the past, change your focus. If you're living in the past, it's time to stop living there (Isaiah 43:18-19).

When Mistakes Are Made

Therefore, if anyone is in Christ, he is a new creation;
the old has gone, the new has come!
2 Corinthians 5:17 NIV

As parents, we are far from perfect. And, without question, our children are imperfect as well. Thus, we are imperfect parents raising imperfect children, and, as a result, mistakes are bound to happen.

Has someone in your family experienced a recent setback? If so, it's time to start looking for the lesson that God is trying to teach. It's time to learn what needs to be learned, change what needs to be changed, and move on.

You and your loved ones should view mistakes as opportunities to reassess God's will for your lives. And while you're at it, you should consider life's inevitable disappointments to be powerful opportunities to learn more—more about yourselves, more about your circumstances, and more about your world.

Father, take our mistakes and turn them into opportunities.

Max Lucado

God is able to take mistakes, when they are committed to Him, and make of them something for our good and for His glory.

Ruth Bell Graham

Mistakes offer the possibility for redemption and a new start in God's kingdom. No matter what you're guilty of, God can restore your innocence.

Barbara Johnson

A PRAYER FOR MOMS

Lord, sometimes I make mistakes and fall short of Your commandments. When I do, forgive me, Father. And help me learn from my mistakes so that I can be a better servant to You and a better example to my family and friends. Amen

I want to become a wiser, more thoughtful person. Where can I go to find wisdom?

THE QUICK ANSWER

If you own a Bible, you have ready access to God's wisdom. Your job is to read, to understand, and to apply His teachings to your life . . . starting now and ending never.

Real Wisdom

Do you want to be counted wise, to build a reputation for wisdom?
Here's what you do: Live well, live wisely, live humbly.
It's the way you live, not the way you talk, that counts.
James 3:13 MSG

Do you seek wisdom for yourself and for your family? Of course you do. But as a savvy mom, you know that wisdom can be an elusive commodity in today's troubled world. In a society filled with temptations and distractions; it's easy for parents and children alike to stray far from the source of the ultimate wisdom: God's Holy Word.

When you begin a daily study of God's Word and live according to His commandments, you will become wise . . . in time. But don't expect to open your Bible today and be wise tomorrow. Wisdom is not like a mushroom; it does not spring up overnight. It is, instead, like an oak tree that starts as a tiny acorn, grows into a sapling, and eventually reaches up to the sky, tall and strong.

Today and every day, study God's Word and live by it. In time, you will accumulate a storehouse of wisdom that will enrich your own life and the lives of your family members, your friends, and the world.

No matter how many books you read, no matter how many schools you attend, you're never really wise until you start making wise choices.

Marie T. Freeman

Wisdom is knowledge applied. Head knowledge is useless on the battlefield. Knowledge stamped on the heart makes one wise.

Beth Moore

A PRAYER FOR MOMS

Dear Lord, give me wisdom to love my family, to care for them, to teach them, and to lead them. Make me wise in Your ways and in Your Holy Word. Let me share Your wisdom through words and deeds, today and every day that I live. Amen

What does the Bible say about the power of faith?

THE QUICK ANSWER

Faith in God is contagious . . . and when it comes to your family's spiritual journey, no one's faith is more contagious than yours! Act, pray, praise, and trust God with the certain knowledge that your friends and family are watching . . . carefully!

The Hem of His Garment

Now faith is being sure of what we hope for
and certain of what we do not see.
Hebrews 11:1 NIV

A suffering woman sought healing in an unusual way: she simply touched the hem of Jesus' garment. When she did, Jesus turned and said, "Daughter, be of good comfort; thy faith hath made thee whole" (Matthew 9:22 KJV). We, too, can be made whole when we place our faith completely and unwaveringly in the person of Jesus Christ.

Concentration camp survivor Corrie ten Boom relied on faith during ten months of imprisonment and torture. Later, despite the fact that four of her family members had died in

Nazi death camps, Corrie's faith was unshaken. She wrote, "There is no pit so deep that God's love is not deeper still." Christians take note: Genuine faith in God means faith in all circumstances, happy or sad, joyful or tragic.

When you place your faith, your trust, indeed your life in the hands of Christ Jesus, you'll be amazed at the marvelous things He can do with you and through you. So strengthen your faith through praise, through worship, through Bible study, and through prayer. Then, trust God's plans. Your Heavenly Father is standing at the door of your heart. If you reach out to Him in faith, He will give you peace and heal your broken spirit. Be content to touch even the smallest fragment of the Master's garment, and He will make you whole.

Faith does not concern itself with the entire journey. One step is enough.

Mrs. Charles E. Cowman

A PRAYER FOR MOMS

Lord, help me to be a mother whose faith is evident to my family and friends. Help me to remember that You are always near and that You can overcome any challenge. With Your love and Your power, Lord, I will live courageously and share my faith with others, today and every day. Amen

QUESTION 26

We live in a materialistic world. What does the Bible have to say about that?

THE QUICK ANSWER

Too much stuff doesn't ensure happiness. In fact, having too much stuff can actually prevent happiness.

To Shop or Not to Shop?

No one can serve two masters. The person will hate one master and love the other, or will follow one master and refuse to follow the other. You cannot serve both God and worldly riches.
Matthew 6:24 NCV

In the demanding world in which we live, financial prosperity can be a good thing, but spiritual prosperity is profoundly more important. Yet our society leads us to believe otherwise. The world glorifies material possessions, personal fame, and physical beauty above all else; these things, of course, are totally unimportant to God. God sees the human heart, and that's what is important to Him.

As you establish your priorities for the coming day, remember this: The world will do everything it can to convince you that "things" are important. The world will tempt you to value fortune above faith and possessions above peace. God, on the other hand, will try to convince you that your relationship with Him is all-important. Trust God.

It's sobering to contemplate how much time, effort, sacrifice, compromise, and attention we give to acquiring and increasing our supply of something that is totally insignificant in eternity.

Anne Graham Lotz

As faithful stewards of what we have, ought we not to give earnest thought to our staggering surplus?

Elisabeth Elliot

The more we stuff ourselves with material pleasures, the less we seem to appreciate life.

Barbara Johnson

A PRAYER FOR MOMS

Dear Lord, keep me mindful that material possessions cannot bring me joy—my joy comes from You. I will share that joy with family, with friends, and with neighbors, this day and every day. Amen

QUESTION 27

What does the Bible say about the way I should manage my time? And what about the amount of time I spend with my family?

THE QUICK ANSWER

The Bible warns us that there's no time to waste. Every day—indeed every moment—is precious.

Time:
A Treasure from God

So teach us to number our days,
that we may gain a heart of wisdom.
Psalm 90:12 NKJV

As every mother knows all too well, there simply isn't enough time to do everything we want—and need—to do. That's why, as mothers, we should be so very careful about the ways that we choose to spend the time that God has given us.

Time is a nonrenewable gift from the Creator. But sometimes, we treat our time here on earth as if it were not a gift at all: We may be tempted to invest our lives in petty diversions or in trivial pursuits. But our Father in heaven beckons each of us to a higher calling.

An important element of our stewardship to God is the way that we choose to spend the time He has entrusted to us. Each waking moment holds the potential to do a good deed, to say a kind word, or to offer a heartfelt prayer. Our challenge, as believers, is to use our time wisely in the service of God's work and in accordance with His plan for our lives.

Each day is a special treasure to be savored and celebrated. May we—as Christian moms who have so much to celebrate—never fail to praise our Creator by rejoicing in this glorious day, and by using it wisely.

There were endless demands on Jesus' time. Still he was able to make that amazing claim of "completing the work you gave me to do." (John 17:4 NIV)

Elisabeth Elliot

The best use of life is love. The best expression of love is time. The best time to love is now.

Rick Warren

A PRAYER FOR MOMS

Dear Lord, You have given me a wonderful gift: time here on earth. Let me use it wisely—for the glory of Your kingdom and the betterment of my family—today and every day that I live. Amen

I have challenges that seem overwhelming at times. What should I do?

THE QUICK ANSWER

Remember that whatever the size of your challenge, God is bigger. Trust Him to solve the problems that are simply too big for you to tackle.

God Can Handle It

For I, the Lord your God, hold your right hand and say to you:
Do not fear, I will help you.
Isaiah 41:13 HCSB

It's a promise that is made over and over again in the Bible: Whatever "it" is, God can handle it.

Life isn't always easy. Far from it! Sometimes, life can be very, very tough. But even then, even during our darkest moments, we're protected by a loving Heavenly Father. When we're worried, God can reassure us; when we're sad, God can comfort us. When our hearts are broken, God is not just near, He is here. So we must lift our thoughts and prayers to Him. When we do, He will answer our prayers. Why? Because He is our Shepherd, and He has promised to protect us now and forever.

God uses our most stumbling, faltering faith-steps as the open door to His doing for us "more than we ask or think."

Catherine Marshall

God is always sufficient in perfect proportion to our need.

Beth Moore

God's saints in all ages have realized that God was enough for them. God is enough for time; God is enough for eternity. God is enough!

Hannah Whitall Smith

God will call you to obey Him and do whatever He asks of you. However, you do not need to be doing something to feel fulfilled. You are fulfilled completely in a relationship with God. When you are filled with Him, what else do you need?

Henry Blackaby and Claude King

A PRAYER FOR MOMS

Dear Lord, whatever "it" is, You can handle it! Let me turn to You when I am fearful or worried. You are my loving Heavenly Father, sufficient in all things and I will always trust You. Amen

Some days are more difficult than others. When times are tough, what should I do?

THE QUICK ANSWER

Difficult days come and go. Stay the course. The sun is shining somewhere and will soon shine on you.

Those Difficult Days

We are pressured in every way but not crushed;
we are perplexed but not in despair.
2 Corinthians 4:8 HCSB

As every mother knows, some days are just plain difficult. Every mother faces days when the baby is sick, when the laundry is piled high, and the bills are piled even higher.

When we find ourselves overtaken by the inevitable frustrations of life, we must catch ourselves, take a deep breath, and lift our thoughts upward. Although we are here on earth struggling to rise above the distractions of the day, we need never struggle alone. God is here—eternal and faithful—and, if we reach out to Him, He will restore perspective and peace to our souls.

Sometimes even the most devout Christian moms can become discouraged, and you are no exception. After all, you live in a world where expectations can be high and demands can be even higher.

If you find yourself enduring difficult circumstances, remember that God remains in His heaven. If you become discouraged with the direction of your day or your life, take a moment to offer your thoughts and prayers to Him. He is a God of possibility, not negativity. He will guide you through your difficulties and beyond them.

When the hard times of life come, we know that no matter how tragic the circumstances seem, no matter how long the spiritual drought, no matter how long and dark the days, the sun is sure to break through; the dawn will come.

Gloria Gaither

When life is difficult, God wants us to have a faith that trusts and waits.

Kay Arthur

A PRAYER FOR MOMS

Dear Lord, when the day is difficult, give me perspective and faith. When I am weak, give me strength. Let me trust in Your promises, Father, and let me live with the assurance that You are with me not only today, but also throughout all eternity. Amen

When I'm disappointed with the way things have turned out, what should I do?

THE QUICK ANSWER

Don't spend too much time asking "Why me, Lord?" Instead, ask, "What now, Lord?" and then get to work. When you do, you'll feel much better.

Beyond Discouragement

But as for you, be strong; don't be discouraged,
for your work has a reward.
2 Chronicles 15:7 HCSB

We Christians have many reasons to celebrate. God is in His heaven; Christ has risen, and we are the sheep of His flock. Yet sometimes, even the most devout Christian women can become discouraged. After all, we live in a world where expectations can be high and demands can be even higher. If you become discouraged with the direction of your day or your life, turn your thoughts and prayers to God. He is a God of possibility, not negativity. He will help you count your blessings instead of your hardships. And then, with a renewed spirit of optimism and hope, you can properly thank your Father in heaven for His blessings, for His love, and for His Son.

God does not dispense strength and encouragement like a druggist fills your prescription. The Lord doesn't promise to give us something to take so we can handle our weary moments. He promises us Himself. That is all. And that is enough.

Charles Swindoll

Overcoming discouragement is simply a matter of taking away the DIS and adding the EN.

Barbara Johnson

Working in the vineyard, working all the day, never be discouraged, only watch and pray.

Fanny Crosby

A PRAYER FOR MOMS

Heavenly Father, when I am discouraged, I will turn to You, and I will also turn to my Christian friends. I thank You, Father, for friends and family members who are willing to encourage me. I will acknowledge their encouragement, and I will share it. Amen

What does the Bible say about eternal life?

THE QUICK ANSWER

God offers you a priceless gift: the gift of eternal life. If you have not already done so, accept God's gift today—tomorrow may be too late.

The Gift of Eternal Life

For God so loved the world that he gave his only Son,
so that everyone who believes in him will not perish
but have eternal life.

John 3:16 NLT

Your life here on earth is merely a preparation for a far different life to come: the eternal life that God promises to those who welcome His Son into their hearts.

As a mere mortal, your vision for the future is finite. God's vision is not burdened by such limitations: His plans extend throughout all eternity. Thus, God's plans for you are not limited to the ups and downs of everyday life. Your Heavenly Father has bigger things in mind . . . much bigger things.

As you struggle with the inevitable hardships and occasional disappointments of life, remember that God has invited you to accept His abundance not only for today but also for all eternity. So keep things in perspective. Although you will inevitably encounter occasional defeats in this world, you'll have all eternity to celebrate the ultimate victory in the next.

The gift of God is eternal life, spiritual life, abundant life through faith in Jesus Christ, the Living Word of God.

Anne Graham Lotz

I can still hardly believe it. I, with shriveled, bent fingers, atrophied muscles, gnarled knees, and no feeling from the shoulders down, will one day have a new body—light, bright and clothed in righteousness—powerful and dazzling.

Joni Eareckson Tada

God loves you and wants you to experience peace and life—abundant and eternal.

Billy Graham

A PRAYER FOR MOMS

Lord, You have given me the gift of eternal life through Christ Jesus. I praise You for that priceless gift. Because I am saved, I will share the story of Your Son and the glory of my salvation with a world that desperately needs Your grace. Amen

Sometimes it's hard for me to forgive the people who have hurt me. What does the Bible say about that?

THE QUICK ANSWER

God's Word instructs you to forgive others . . . no exceptions. Forgiveness is its own reward and bitterness is its own punishment. So guard your words and your thoughts accordingly.

Forgiveness Now

Be gentle with one another, sensitive. Forgive one another as quickly and thoroughly as God in Christ forgave you.
Ephesians 4:32 MSG

Even the most mild-mannered moms will, on occasion, have reason to become angry with the inevitable shortcomings of family members and friends. But wise women are quick to forgive others, just as God has forgiven them.

Forgiveness is God's commandment, but oh how difficult a commandment it can be to follow. Being frail, fallible, imperfect human beings, we are quick to anger, quick to blame, slow to forgive, and even slower to forget. No matter. Even when forgiveness is difficult, God's Word is clear.

If, in your heart, you hold bitterness against even a single person, forgive. If there exists even one person, alive or dead, whom you have not forgiven, follow God's commandment and His will for your life: forgive. If you are embittered against yourself for some past mistake or shortcoming, forgive. Then, to the best of your abilities, forget, and move on. Bitterness and regret are not part of God's plan for your life. Forgiveness is.

———————————

God expects us to forgive others as He has forgiven us; we are to follow His example by having a forgiving heart.

Vonette Bright

Grudges are like hand grenades; it is wise to release them before they destroy you.

Barbara Johnson

A PRAYER FOR MOMS

Lord, I know that I need to forgive others just as You have forgiven me. Help me to be an example of forgiveness to my children. Keep me mindful, Father, that I am never fully liberated until I have been freed from the chains of bitterness—and that You offer me that freedom through Your Son, Christ Jesus. Amen

QUESTION 33

What does the Bible say about physical fitness?

THE QUICK ANSWER

God's Word teaches that your body is a miraculous gift from the Creator, and you should treat it that way.

Fitness Matters

Whatever you eat or drink or whatever you do,
you must do all for the glory of God.
1 Corinthians 10:31 NLT

Are you shaping up or spreading out? Do you eat sensibly and exercise regularly, or do you spend most of your time on the couch with a Twinkie in one hand and a clicker in the other? Are you choosing to treat your body like a temple or a trash heap? How you answer these questions will help determine how long you live and how well you live.

Physical fitness is a choice, a choice that requires discipline—it's as simple as that. So, do yourself this favor: treat your body like a one-of-a-kind gift from God . . . because that's precisely what your body is.

God wants you to give Him your body. Some people do foolish things with their bodies. God wants your body as a holy sacrifice.

Warren Wiersbe

Our primary motivation should not be for more energy or to avoid a heart attack but to please God with our bodies.

Carole Lewis

People are funny. When they are young, they will spend their health to get wealth. Later, they will gladly pay all they have trying to get their health back.

John Maxwell

You can't buy good health at the doctor's office—you've got to earn it for yourself.

Marie T. Freeman

A PRAYER FOR MOMS

Lord, all that I am belongs to You. As I serve You with all that I am and all that I have, help me to honor You by caring for the body that You have given me. Amen.

Sometimes it's hard to be a patient parent. What advice can I find in God's Word?

THE QUICK ANSWER

God's Word teaches that patience is better than strength (Proverbs 16:32). So wise parents learn to control anger before anger controls them.

Patience NOW!

A patient person [shows] great understanding,
but a quick-tempered one promotes foolishness.
Proverbs 14:29 HCSB

The rigors of motherhood can test the patience of the most even-tempered moms: From time to time, even the most mannerly children may do things that worry us or confuse us or anger us. Why? Because they are children, and because they are human.

As loving parents, we must be patient with our children's shortcomings (just as they, too, must be patient with our own). But our patience must not be restricted to those who live under our care. We must also strive, to the best of our abilities, to exercise patience in all our dealings, because our children are watching and learning.

Sometimes, patience is simply the price we pay for being responsible parents, and that's exactly as it should be. After all, think how patient our Heavenly Father has been with us.

Let me encourage you to continue to wait with faith. God may not perform a miracle, but He is trustworthy to touch you and make you whole where there used to be a hole.

Lisa Whelchel

He makes us wait. He keeps us in the dark on purpose. He makes us walk when we want to run, sit still when we want to walk, for he has things to do in our souls that we are not interested in.

Elisabeth Elliot

Waiting is an essential part of spiritual discipline. It can be the ultimate test of faith.

Anne Graham Lotz

A PRAYER FOR MOMS

Heavenly Father, let me wait quietly for You. Let me live according to Your plan and according to Your timetable. When I am hurried, slow me down. When I become impatient with others, give me empathy. Today, I want to be a patient Christian, Dear Lord, as I trust in You and in Your master plan. Amen

QUESTION 35

Sometimes I have doubts about my future and doubts about my faith. What should I do?

THE QUICK ANSWER

When you have doubts, it is important to take those doubts to the Lord.

When You Have Doubts

Now if any of you lacks wisdom, he should ask God, who gives to all generously and without criticizing, and it will be given to him. But let him ask in faith without doubting. For the doubter is like the surging sea, driven and tossed by the wind.
James 1:5-6 HCSB

If you've never had any doubts about your faith, then you can stop reading this page now and skip to the next. But if you've ever been plagued by doubts about your faith or your God, keep reading.

Even some of the most faithful Christians are, at times, beset by occasional bouts of discouragement and doubt. But even when we feel far removed from God, God is never far removed from us. He is always with us, always willing to calm the storms of life—always willing to replace our doubts with comfort and assurance.

Whenever you're plagued by doubts, that's precisely the moment you should seek God's presence by genuinely seeking to establish a deeper, more meaningful relationship with His Son. Then you may rest assured that in time, God will calm your fears, answer your prayers, and restore your confidence.

Mark it down. God never turns away the honest seeker. Go to God with your questions. You may not find all the answers, but in finding God, you know the One who does.

Max Lucado

We are most vulnerable to the piercing winds of doubt when we distance ourselves from the mission and fellowship to which Christ has called us.

Joni Eareckson Tada

Unconfessed sin in your life will cause you to doubt.

Anne Graham Lotz

A PRAYER FOR MOMS

Dear Lord, when I am filled with uncertainty and doubt, give me faith. In the dark moments of life, keep me mindful of Your healing power and Your infinite love, so that I may live courageously and faithfully today and every day. Amen

Sometimes, when I'm supposed to be having fun, I feel guilty. What does the Bible say about fun?

THE QUICK ANSWER

Today and every day, God wants you to rejoice. In fact, He teaches us that every day is a cause for celebration: So don't feel guilty about having good, clean fun. As long as you're following in the footsteps of His Son, God approves.

Time for Fun

So I recommend having fun, because there is nothing better for people to do in this world than to eat, drink, and enjoy life. That way they will experience some happiness along with all the hard work God gives them.
Ecclesiastes 8:15 NLT

Are you a woman who takes time each day to really enjoy life? Hopefully so. After all, you are the recipient of a precious gift—the gift of life. And because God has seen fit to give you this gift, it is incumbent upon you to use it and to enjoy it. But sometimes, amid the inevitable pressures of everyday living, really enjoying life may seem almost impossible. It is not.

For most of us, fun is as much a function of attitude as it is a function of environment. So whether you're standing victorious atop one of life's mountains or trudging through one of life's valleys, enjoy yourself. You deserve to have fun today, and God wants you to have fun today . . . so what on earth are you waiting for?

Our thoughts, not our circumstances, determine our happiness.

John Maxwell

Whence comes this idea that if what we are doing is fun, it can't be God's will? The God who made giraffes, a baby's fingernails, a puppy's tail, a crooknecked squash, the bobwhite's call, and a young girl's giggle, has a sense of humor. Make no mistake about that.

Catherine Marshall

Smile—it increases your face value.

Anonymous

A PRAYER FOR MOMS

Lord, make me a happy Christian. Let me rejoice in the gift of this day, and let me praise You for the gift of Your Son. Make me be a joyful mother, Lord, as I share Your Good News with all those who need Your healing touch. Amen

What does God's Word say about work?

THE QUICK ANSWER

Work is honored by God—He expects each of us to do our fair share. So encourage your children to find meaningful work that they enjoy. People who are passionate about their professions are usually more successful than people who aren't.

No Shortcuts

In all the work you are doing, work the best you can.
Work as if you were doing it for the Lord, not for people.
Colossians 3:23 NCV

Providing for a family requires work, and lots of it. And whether or not your work carries you outside the home, your good works have earned the gratitude of your loved ones and the praise of your Heavenly Father.

It has been said that there are no shortcuts to any place worth going. Mothers agree. Making the grade in today's competitive workplace is not easy. In fact, it can be very difficult indeed. The same can be said for the important work that occurs within the four walls of your home.

God did not create you and your family for lives of mediocrity; He created you for far greater things. Accomplishing God's work is seldom easy. What's required is determination, persistence, patience, and discipline—which is perfectly fine with God. After all, He knows that you're up to the task, and He has big plans for all of you. Very big plans . . .

Christian work is any kind of work, from cleaning a sewer to preaching a sermon, that is done by a Christian and offered to God.

Elisabeth Elliot

Great relief and satisfaction can come from seeking God's priorities for us in each season, discerning what is "best" in the midst of many noble opportunities, and pouring our most excellent energies into those things.

Beth Moore

A PRAYER FOR MOMS

Heavenly Father, You know that motherhood is difficult work. When I am tired, give me strength. When I become frustrated, give me patience. When I lose sight of Your purpose for my life, give me a passion for my daily responsibilities. Let me raise my children to be Your loving, faithful servants, and let all the honor and glory be Yours. Amen

Sometimes life is difficult. When I'm fearful for myself or my family, what should I do?

THE QUICK ANSWER

Ask God for strength and wisdom. And above all, trust the Lord to solve problems that are simply too big for you to solve. When you turn everything over to God, you can live courageously.

Living Courageously

The Lord is the One who will go before you.
He will be with you; He will not leave you or forsake you.
Do not be afraid or discouraged.
Deuteronomy 31:8 HCSB

This world can be a dangerous and daunting place, but Christians have every reason to live courageously. After all, the ultimate battle has already been fought and won on the cross at Calvary. But even the most dedicated Christian mom may find her courage tested by the inevitable disappointments and fears that visit the lives of believers and non-believers alike.

The next time you find your courage tested to the limit, remember to take your fears to God. If you call upon Him, you will be comforted. Whatever your challenge, whatever your trouble, God can handle it. And will.

―――――――――――

What is courage? It is the ability to be strong in trust, in conviction, in obedience. To be courageous is to step out in faith—to trust and obey, no matter what.

Kay Arthur

If a person fears God, he or she has no reason to fear anything else. On the other hand, if a person does not fear God, then fear becomes a way of life.

Beth Moore

When once we are assured that God is good, then there can be nothing left to fear.

Hannah Whitall Smith

A PRAYER FOR MOMS

Lord, at times, this world is a fearful place. I fear for my family and especially for my children. Yet, You have promised me that You are with me always. With You as my protector, I am not afraid. Today, Dear Lord, let me live courageously as I place my trust in You. Amen

Sometimes, the demands of life can wear me down and wear me out. What does the Bible say about renewing my strength?

THE QUICK ANSWER

God can make all things new, including you. When you are weak or worried, God can renew your spirit. Your task is to let Him.

Running on Empty

I will give you a new heart and put a new spirit in you . . . .
Ezekiel 36:26 NIV

God intends that His children lead joyous lives filled with abundance and peace. But sometimes, as all mothers can attest, abundance and peace seem very far away. It is then that we must turn to God for renewal, and when we do, He will restore us.

Have you "tapped in" to the power of God, or are you muddling along under your own power? If you are weary, worried, fretful, or fearful, then it is time to turn to a strength much greater than your own.

The Bible tells us that we can do all things through the power of our risen Savior, Jesus Christ. Our challenge, then, is clear. We must place Christ where He belongs: at the very center of our lives.

Are you tired or troubled? Turn your heart toward God in prayer. Are you weak or worried? Make the time to delve deeply into God's Holy Word. When you do, you'll discover that the Creator of the universe stands ready and able to create a new sense of wonderment and joy in you.

If you're willing to repair your life, God is willing to help. If you're not willing to repair your life, God is willing to wait.

Marie T. Freeman

But while relaxation is one thing, refreshment is another. We need to drink frequently and at length from God's fresh springs, to spend time in the Scripture, time in fellowship with Him, time worshiping Him.

Ruth Bell Graham

A PRAYER FOR MOMS

Lord, I am an imperfect mother. Sometimes, I become overwhelmed by the demands of the day. When I feel tired or discouraged, renew my strength. When I am worried, let me turn my thoughts and my prayers to You. Let me trust Your promises, Dear Lord, and let me accept Your unending love, now and forever. Amen

QUESTION 40

What does God's Word say about generosity?

THE QUICK ANSWER

The Bible teaches us that generosity is its own reward. So, would you like to be a little happier? Try sharing a few more of the blessings that God has bestowed upon you. In other words, if you want to be happy, be generous. And if you want to be unhappy, be greedy.

The Wisdom to Be Generous

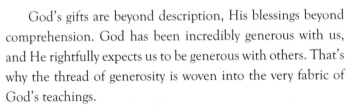

Freely you have received, freely give.
Matthew 10:8 NIV

God's gifts are beyond description, His blessings beyond comprehension. God has been incredibly generous with us, and He rightfully expects us to be generous with others. That's why the thread of generosity is woven into the very fabric of God's teachings.

In the Old Testament, we are told that, "The good person is generous and lends lavishly..." (Psalm 112:5 MSG). And in the New Testament we are instructed, "Freely you have received, freely give" (Matthew 10:8 NKJV). These principles still apply.

As we establish priorities for our days and our lives, we are advised to give freely of our time, our possessions, and our love—just as God has given freely to us.

Of course, we can never fully repay God for His gifts, but we can share them with others. And we should.

Nothing is really ours until we share it.

C. S. Lewis

The measure of a life, after all, is not its duration but its donation.

Corrie ten Boom

We can't do everything, but can we do anything more valuable than invest ourselves in another?

Elisabeth Elliot

The test of generosity is not how much you give, but how much you have left.

Anonymous

A PRAYER FOR MOMS

Lord, make me a generous and cheerful Christian. Let me be kind to those who need my encouragement, and let me share with those who need my help, today and every day. Amen

QUESTION 41

What does the Bible say about following in Jesus' footsteps?

THE QUICK ANSWER

If you want to follow in Christ's footsteps . . . welcome Him into your heart, obey His commandments, and share His never-ending love.

Following Jesus

Whoever serves me must follow me.
Then my servant will be with me everywhere I am.
My Father will honor anyone who serves me.
John 12:26 NCV

Jesus walks with you. Are you walking with Him? Hopefully, you will choose to walk with Him today and every day of your life. And hopefully, you will encourage your family to do the same.

God's Word is clear: When we genuinely invite Christ to reign over our hearts, and when we accept His transforming love, we are forever changed. When we welcome Christ into our hearts, an old life ends and a new way of living—along with a completely new way of viewing the world—begins.

Each morning offers a fresh opportunity to invite Christ, yet once again, to rule over our hearts and our days. Each morning presents yet another opportunity to take up His cross and follow in His footsteps. Today, let us rejoice in the new life that is ours through Christ, and let us follow Him, step by step, on the path that He first walked.

It's your heart that Jesus longs for: your will to be made His own with self on the cross forever, and Jesus alone on the throne.

Ruth Bell Graham

Jesus challenges you and me to keep our focus daily on the cross of His will if we want to be His disciples.

Anne Graham Lotz

Will you, with a glad and eager surrender, hand yourself and all that concerns you over into his hands? If you will do this, your soul will begin to know something of the joy of union with Christ.

Hannah Whitall Smith

A PRAYER FOR MOMS

Dear Lord, You sent Jesus to save the world and to save me. I thank You for Jesus, and I will do my best to follow Him, today and forever. Amen

Sometimes I feel like my problems are simply too big for me to handle. What should I do?

THE QUICK ANSWER

Remember that the Lord is your Shepherd today, tomorrow, and forever.

Trust the Shepherd

The Lord is my shepherd; I shall not want.

Psalm 23:1 KJV

In the 23rd Psalm, David teaches us that God is like a watchful Shepherd caring for His flock. No wonder these verses have provided comfort and hope for generations of believers.

You are precious in the eyes of God. You are His priceless creation, made in His image, and protected by Him. God watches over every step you make and every breath you take, so you need never be afraid. But sometimes, fear has a way of slipping into the minds and hearts of even the most devout believers—and you are no exception.

As a busy woman, you know from firsthand experience that life is not always easy. But as a recipient of God's grace, you also know that you are protected by a loving Heavenly Father.

On occasion, you will confront circumstances that trouble you to the very core of your soul. When you are afraid, trust in God. When you are worried, turn your concerns over to Him. When you are anxious, be still and listen for the quiet assurance of God's promises. And then, place your life in His hands. He is your Shepherd today and throughout eternity. Trust the Shepherd.

Christ reigns in his church as shepherd-king. He has supremacy, but it is the superiority of a wise and tender shepherd over his needy and loving flock. He commands and receives obedience, but it is willing obedience of well-cared-for-sheep, offered joyfully to their beloved Shepherd, whose voice they know so well. He rules by the force of love and the energy of goodness.

C. H. Spurgeon

You can better understand the 23rd Psalm when you are acquainted with The Shepherd.

Anonymous

A PRAYER FOR MOMS

Lord, You are my Shepherd. You care for me; You comfort me; You watch over me; and You have saved me. I will praise You, Father, for Your glorious works, for Your protection, for Your love, and for Your Son. Amen

QUESTION 43

If I want God to guide me, what should I do?

THE QUICK ANSWER

If you want God's guidance, ask for it. When you pray for guidance, God will give it.

God's Guidance

The LORD says, "I will guide you along the best pathway
for your life. I will advise you and watch over you."
Psalm 32:8 NLT

The Bible promises that God will guide you if you let Him. Your job, of course, is to let Him. But sometimes, you will be tempted to do otherwise. Sometimes, you'll be tempted to go along with the crowd; other times, you'll be tempted to do things your way, not God's way. When you feel those temptations, resist them.

What will you allow to guide you through the coming day: your own desires (or, for that matter, the desires of your friends)? Or will you allow God to lead the way? The answer should be obvious. You should let God be your guide. When you entrust your life to Him completely and without reservation, God will give you the strength to meet any challenge, the courage to face any trial, and the wisdom to live in His righteousness. So trust Him today and seek His guidance. When you do, your next step will be the right one.

———————————

We have ample evidence that the Lord is able to guide. The promises cover every imaginable situation. All we need to do is to take the hand he stretches out.

Elisabeth Elliot

If we neglect the Bible, we cannot expect to benefit from the wisdom and direction that result from knowing God's Word.

Vonette Bright

Are you serious about wanting God's guidance to become a personal reality in your life? The first step is to tell God that you know you can't manage your own life; that you need his help.

Catherine Marshall

A PRAYER FOR MOMS

Dear Lord, today I will trust You more completely. I will lean upon Your understanding, not mine. And I will trust You to guide my steps along a path of Your choosing. Amen

QUESTION 44

I'm a very busy mother with a very full to-do list. What should I do.

THE QUICK ANSWER

Do first things first, and keep your focus on high-priority tasks. And remember this: your highest priority should be your relationship with God and His Son.

Too Busy?

Come to Me, all you who are weary and burdened, and I will give you rest. Take My yoke upon you and learn from Me, because I am gentle and humble in heart, and you will find rest for your souls. For My yoke is easy and My burden is light.
Matthew 11:28-30 HCSB

If you're a mom with too many responsibilities and too few hours in which to fulfill them, you are not alone. Motherhood is so demanding that sometimes you may feel as if you have no time for yourself . . . and no time for God.

Has the busy pace of life robbed you of the peace that might otherwise be yours through Jesus Christ? If so, you are simply too busy for your own good. Through His Son Jesus, God offers you a peace that passes human understanding, but He won't force His peace upon you; in order to experience it, you must slow down long enough to sense His presence and His love.

Today, as a gift to yourself, to your family, and to the world, slow down long enough to claim the inner peace that is your spiritual birthright: the peace of Jesus Christ. It is offered freely; it has been paid for in full; it is yours for the asking. So ask. And then share.

In our tense, uptight society where folks are rushing to make appointments they have already missed, a good laugh can be as refreshing as a cup of cold water in the desert.

Barbara Johnson

If you can't seem to find time for God, then you're simply too busy for your own good. God is never too busy for you, and you should never be too busy for Him.

Marie T. Freeman

A PRAYER FOR MOMS

Dear Lord, sometimes, I am distracted by the busyness of the day or the demands of the moment. When I am worried or anxious, Father, turn my thoughts back to You. Help me to trust Your will, to follow Your commands, and to accept Your peace, today and forever. Amen

If I feel guilty about something, what should I do?

THE QUICK ANSWER

First, make sure that you're no longer doing the thing that caused your guilt in the first place. Then, ask for forgiveness (from God and from anybody you've hurt). Next, make sure to forgive yourself. And finally, if you still have residual feelings of bitterness or regret, keep asking God to cleanse your heart. When you ask, He will answer in His own time and in His own way.

Beyond Guilt

There is therefore now no condemnation to those
who are in Christ Jesus, who do not walk according to the flesh,
but according to the Spirit.
Romans 8:1 NKJV

All of us have made mistakes. Sometimes our failures result from our own shortsightedness. On other occasions, we are swept up in events that are beyond our abilities to control. Under either set of circumstances, we may experience intense feelings of guilt. But God has an answer for the guilt that we feel. That answer, of course, is His forgiveness.

When we ask our Heavenly Father for His forgiveness, He forgives us completely and without reservation. Then, we must do the difficult work of forgiving ourselves in the same way that God has forgiven us: thoroughly and unconditionally.

If you're feeling guilty, then it's time for a special kind of housecleaning—a housecleaning of your mind and your heart . . . beginning NOW!

If God has forgiven you, why can't you forgive yourself?

Marie T. Freeman

Satan knows that if you live under a dark cloud of guilt, you will not be able to witness effectively or serve the Lord with power and blessing.

Warren Wiersbe

Guilt is a gift that leads us to grace.

Franklin Graham

A PRAYER FOR MOMS

Dear Lord, thank You for the guilt that I feel when I disobey You. Help me confess my wrongdoings, help me accept Your forgiveness, and help me renew my passion to serve You. Amen

Sometimes it's hard to be hopeful. What does the Bible say about hope?

THE QUICK ANSWER

Don't give up hope: Other people have experienced the same kind of hard times you may be experiencing now. They made it, and so can you (Psalm 146:5).

Finding Hope

Now may the God of hope fill you with all joy
and peace in believing, so that you may overflow with hope
by the power of the Holy Spirit.
Romans 15:13 HCSB

Are you a hope-filled mom? You should be. After all, God is good; His love endures; and He has offered you the priceless gift of eternal life. And, of course, God has blessed you with a loving family. But sometimes, in life's darker moments, you may lose sight of those blessings, and when you do, it's easy to lose hope.

When a suffering woman sought healing by merely touching the hem of His cloak, Jesus replied, "Daughter, be of good comfort; thy faith hath made thee whole" (Matthew 9:22

KJV). The message to believers is clear: if we are to be made whole by God, we must live by faith.

If you find yourself falling into the spiritual traps of worry and discouragement, seek the healing touch of Jesus and the encouraging words of fellow Christians. This world can be a place of trials and tribulations, but as believers, we are secure. Our hope is in God; He has promised us peace, joy, and eternal life. And, of course, God keeps His promises today, tomorrow, and forever, amen!

You can look forward with hope, because one day there will be no more separation, no more scars, and no more suffering in My Father's House. It's the home of your dreams!

Anne Graham Lotz

Hope must be in the future tense. Faith, to be faith, must always be in the present tense.

Catherine Marshall

A PRAYER FOR MOMS

Today, Dear Lord, I will live in hope. If I become discouraged, I will turn to You. If I grow weary, I will seek strength in You. In every aspect of my life, I will trust You. You are my Father, Lord, and I place my hope and my faith in You. Amen

What does the Bible have to say about the importance of being a joyful person?

THE QUICK ANSWER

God's Word instructs us to be joyful. And we must remember that joy does not depend upon our circumstances, but upon our relationship with God.

His Joy and Yours

A joyful heart is good medicine,
but a broken spirit dries up the bones.
Proverbs 17:22 NASB

Are you a mom whose smile is evident for all to see? If so, congratulations: your joyful spirit serves as a powerful example to your family and friends. And because of your attitude, you may be assured that your children will indeed "rise up" and call you blessed (Proverbs 31:28).

Sometimes, amid the inevitable hustle and bustle of life here on earth, you may forfeit—albeit temporarily—the joy that God intends for you to experience and to share. But even on life's most difficult days, you may rest assured that God is in His heaven, and He still cares for you.

God's plan for you and your family includes heaping helpings of abundance and joy. Claim them. And remember that Christ offers you and your family priceless gifts: His abundance, His peace, and His joy. Accept those gifts and share them freely, just as Christ has freely shared Himself with you.

What is your focus today? Joy comes when it is Jesus first, others second . . . then you.

Kay Arthur

According to Jesus, it is God's will that His children be filled with the joy of life.

Catherine Marshall

The Christian lifestyle is not one of legalistic do's and don'ts, but one that is positive, attractive, and joyful.

Vonette Bright

A PRAYER FOR MOMS

Dear Lord, You have given me so many blessings; let me celebrate Your gifts. Make me thankful, loving, responsible, and wise. I praise You, Father, for the gift of Your Son and for the priceless gift of salvation. Make me be a joyful Christian and a worthy example to my loved ones, today and every day. Amen

I know I should be kind to other people, but sometimes it's so easy to overlook the needs of others. What does the Bible instruct me to do?

THE QUICK ANSWER

You can't just talk about it: In order to be a kind person, you must not only think kind thoughts, you must also do kind things. So get busy! The time to be kind is now.

Choosing to Be Kind

Our Father is kind; you be kind. "Don't pick on people, jump on their failures, criticize their faults—unless, of course, you want the same treatment. Don't condemn those who are down; that hardness can boomerang. Be easy on people; you'll find life a lot easier."

Luke 6:36-37 MSG

Kindness is a choice. Sometimes, when we feel happy or generous, we find it easy to be kind. Other times, when we are discouraged or tired, we can scarcely summon the energy to utter a single kind word. But, God's commandment is clear: He intends that we make the conscious choice to treat others with kindness and respect, no matter our circumstances, no matter our emotions.

In the busyness and confusion of daily life, it is easy to lose focus, and it is easy to become frustrated. We are imperfect human beings struggling to manage our lives as best we can, but we often fall short. When we are distracted or disappointed, we may neglect to share a kind word or a kind deed. This oversight hurts others, but it hurts us most of all.

Today, slow yourself down and be alert for people who need your smile, your kind words, or your helping hand. Make kindness a centerpiece of your dealings with others. They will be blessed, and you will be too.

If we have the true love of God in our hearts, we will show it in our lives. We will not have to go up and down the earth proclaiming it. We will show it in everything we say or do.

D. L. Moody

Kindness in this world will do much to help others, not only to come into the light, but also to grow in grace day by day.

Fanny Crosby

A PRAYER FOR MOMS

Lord, make me a loving, encouraging Christian mother. And, let my love for Christ be reflected through the kindness that I show to those who need the healing touch of the Master's hand. Amen

What does the Bible say about enthusiasm?

THE QUICK ANSWER

Be enthusiastic about your faith. When you allow yourself to become extremely enthusiastic about your faith, other people will notice—and so will God.

Enthused About Life

Whatever you do, do it enthusiastically,
as something done for the Lord and not for men.
Colossians 3:23 HCSB

Do you see each day as a glorious opportunity to serve God and to do His will? Are you enthused about life, or do you struggle through each day giving scarcely a thought to God's blessings?

If you're a mother with too many demands and too few hours in which to meet them, you are not alone. Motherhood is perhaps the world's most demanding profession. But don't fret. Instead, focus upon God and upon His love for you. Then, ask Him for the strength you need to fulfill your responsibilities. God will give you the energy to do the most important things on today's to-do list . . . if you ask Him. So ask Him.

Catch on fire with enthusiasm and people will come for miles to watch you burn.

John Wesley

Enthusiasm, like the flu, is contagious—we get it from one another.

Barbara Johnson

One of the great needs in the church today is for every Christian to become enthusiastic about his faith in Jesus Christ.

Billy Graham

When we wholeheartedly commit ourselves to God, there is nothing mediocre or run-of-the-mill about us. To live for Christ is to be passionate about our Lord and about our lives.

Jim Gallery

A PRAYER FOR MOMS

Dear Lord, let me be an enthusiastic participant in life. And let my enthusiasm bring honor and glory to You. Amen

Sometimes I'm tempted to give up. What advice does the Bible have for me?

THE QUICK ANSWER

The world encourages instant gratification but God's work takes time. So remember the words of C. H. Spurgeon: "By perseverance, the snail reached the ark."

The Power of Perseverance

I have fought the good fight, I have finished the race,
I have kept the faith.
2 Timothy 4:7 HCSB

Someone once said, "Life is a marathon, not a sprint." The same can be said for motherhood. Motherhood requires courage, perseverance, determination, and, of course, an unending supply of motherly love. Are you tired? Ask God for strength. Are you discouraged? Believe in His promises. Are you frustrated or fearful? Pray as if everything depended upon God, and work as if everything depended upon you. With God's help, you will find the strength to be the kind of mom who makes her Heavenly Father beam with pride.

When you fall and skin your knees and skin your heart, He'll pick you up.

Charles Stanley

Your life is not a boring stretch of highway. It's a straight line to heaven. And just look at the fields ripening along the way. Look at the tenacity and endurance. Look at the grains of righteousness. You'll have quite a crop at harvest . . . so don't give up!

Joni Eareckson Tada

Failure is one of life's most powerful teachers. How we handle our failures determines whether we're going to simply "get by" in life or "press on."

Beth Moore

A PRAYER FOR MOMS

Dear Lord, when my responsibilities as a mother seem overwhelming, slow me down and give me perspective. Keep me steady and sure. When I become weary, let me persevere so that, in Your time, I might finish my work here on earth, and that You might then say, "Well done my good and faithful servant." Amen

Sometimes the truth hurts. What does the Bible say about integrity?

THE QUICK ANSWER

The Bible leaves no room for doubt: Total honesty is the only path for those who seek to follow Christ. Truth sets you free; untruth imprisons you. So measure your words accordingly.

The Best Policy

The honest person will live in safety,
but the dishonest will be caught.
Proverbs 10:9 NCV

It has been said on many occasions and in many ways that honesty is the best policy. For believers, it is far more important to note that honesty is God's policy. And if we are to be servants worthy of Jesus Christ, we must be honest and forthright in our communications with others. Sometimes, honesty is difficult; sometimes, honesty is painful; sometimes, honesty is inconvenient; but honesty is always God's commandment.

In the Book of Proverbs, we read, "The Lord detests lying lips, but he delights in men who are truthful" (12:22 NIV).

Clearly, we must strive to be women whose words are pleasing to our Creator. Truth is God's way, and it must be our way, too, even when telling the truth is difficult. As loving mothers, we can do no less.

Integrity is not a given factor in everyone's life. It is a result of self-discipline, inner trust, and a decision to be relentlessly honest in all situations in our lives.

John Maxwell

The single most important element in any human relationship is honesty—with oneself, with God, and with others.

Catherine Marshall

Much guilt arises in the life of the believer from practicing the chameleon life of environmental adaptation.

Beth Moore

A PRAYER FOR MOMS

Dear Lord, You command Your children to walk in truth. Let me follow Your commandment. Give me the courage to speak honestly, and let me walk righteously with You so that others might see Your eternal truth reflected in my words and my deeds. Amen

Our family has so much to be thankful for. What should we do?

THE QUICK ANSWER

Don't overlook God's gifts: Every sunrise represents yet another beautifully wrapped gift from God. Unwrap it; treasure it; use it; and give thanks to the Giver.

Taking Time to Say "Thanks"

Give thanks to the Lord, for He is good;
His faithful love endures forever.
Psalm 118:29 HCSB

As believing Christians, we are blessed beyond measure. God sent His only Son to die for our sins. And, God has given us the priceless gifts of eternal love and eternal life. We, in turn, are instructed to approach our Heavenly Father with reverence and thanksgiving. But, as busy mothers caught up in the inevitable demands of everyday life, we sometimes fail to pause and thank our Creator for the countless blessings He has bestowed upon us.

When we slow down and express our gratitude to the One who made us, we enrich our own lives and the lives of our loved ones. Thanksgiving should become a habit, a regular part of our daily routines. Yes, God has blessed us beyond measure, and we owe Him everything, including our eternal praise.

God is in control, and therefore in everything I can give thanks, not because of the situation, but because of the One who directs and rules over it.

Kay Arthur

Do you know that if at birth I had been able to make one petition, it would have been that I should be born blind? Because, when I get to heaven, the first face that shall ever gladden my sight will be that of my Savior!

Fanny Crosby

A PRAYER FOR MOMS

Dear Lord, You have blessed me with a loving family—make me a mother who is thankful, loving, responsible, and wise. I praise You, Father, for the gift of Your Son and for the gift of salvation. Let me be a joyful Christian and a worthy example, this day and every day that I live. Amen

It's hard not to be judgmental of other people, and it's hard not to judge their motives. What does the Bible say about judging others?

THE QUICK ANSWER

Your ability to judge others requires a divine insight that you simply don't have. So do everybody (including yourself) a favor: don't judge.

The Wisdom Not to Judge

Do not judge, or you too will be judged.
For in the same way you judge others, you will be judged,
and with the measure you use, it will be measured to you.
Matthew 7:1 NIV

The warning of Matthew 7:1 is clear and simple: "Do not judge." Yet even the most devoted Christians may fall prey to a powerful yet subtle temptation: the temptation to judge others. But as obedient followers of Christ, we are commanded to refrain from such behavior.

As Jesus came upon a young woman who had been condemned by the Pharisees, He spoke not only to the crowd that was gathered there, but also to all generations when He warned, "He that is without sin among you, let him first cast a stone at her" (John 8:7 KJV). Christ's message is clear, and it applies not only to the Pharisees of ancient times, but also to us.

No creed or school of thought can monopolize the Spirit of God.

Oswald Chambers

Judging draws the judgment of others.

Catherine Marshall

Christians think they are prosecuting attorneys or judges, when, in reality, God has called all of us to be witnesses.

Warren Wiersbe

A PRAYER FOR MOMS

Dear Lord, sometimes I am quick to judge others. But, You have commanded me not to judge. Keep me mindful, Father, that when I judge others, I am living outside of Your will for my life. You have forgiven me, Lord. Let me forgive others, let me love them, and let me help them . . . without judging them. Amen

Our family has more blessings than we can count. How should we respond?

THE QUICK ANSWER

To experience the full measure of God's blessings, you must give praise and thanks to the Giver. So make it a point to thank God for His blessings many times each day.

The Wisdom to Be Grateful

Let the message about the Messiah dwell richly among you,
teaching and admonishing one another in all wisdom,
and singing psalms, hymns, and spiritual songs,
with gratitude in your hearts to God.
Colossians 3:16 HCSB

For most of us, life is busy and complicated. We have countless responsibilities, some of which begin before sunrise and many of which end long after sunset. Amid the rush and crush of the daily grind, it is easy to lose sight of God and His blessings. But, when we forget to slow down and say "Thank You" to our Maker, we rob ourselves of His presence, His peace, and His joy.

Our task—as the leaders of our families and as believing Christians—is to praise God many times each day. Then, with gratitude in our hearts, we can face our daily duties with the perspective and power that only He can provide.

If you won't fill your heart with gratitude, the devil will fill it with something else.

Marie T. Freeman

Gratitude changes the pangs of memory into a tranquil joy.

Dietrich Bonhoeffer

Think of the blessings we so easily take for granted: Life itself; preservation from danger; every bit of health we enjoy; every hour of liberty; the ability to see, to hear, to speak, to think, and to imagine all this comes from the hand of God.

Billy Graham

A PRAYER FOR MOMS

Lord, let my attitude be one of gratitude. You have given me much; when I think of Your grace and goodness, I am humbled and thankful. Today, let me express my thanksgiving, Father, not just through my words but also through my deeds . . . and may all the glory be Yours. Amen

I've developed some bad habits. What should I do?

THE QUICK ANSWER

Target your most unhealthy habit first, and attack it with vigor. When it comes to defeating harmful habitual behaviors, you'll need focus, determination, prayer, more focus, more determination, and more prayer.

Healthy Habits

Do not be deceived: "Evil company corrupts good habits."
1 Corinthians 15:33 NKJV

It's an old saying and a true one: First, you make your habits, and then your habits make you. Some habits will inevitably bring you closer to God; other habits will lead you away from the path He has chosen for you. If you sincerely desire to improve your spiritual health, you must honestly examine the habits that make up the fabric of your day. And you must abandon those habits that are displeasing to God.

If you trust God, and if you keep asking for His help, He can transform your life. If you sincerely ask Him to help you, the same God who created the universe will help you defeat the harmful habits that have heretofore defeated you. So, if at first you don't succeed, keep praying. God is listening, and He's ready to help you become a better person if you ask Him . . . so ask today.

Since behaviors become habits, make them work with you and not against you.

E. Stanley Jones

Prayer is a habit. Worship is a habit. Kindness is a habit. And if you want to please God, you'd better make sure that these habits are your habits.

Marie T. Freeman

You will never change your life until you change something you do daily.

John Maxwell

Sow an act, and you reap a habit. Sow a habit and you reap a character. Sow a character and you reap a destiny.

Anonymous

A PRAYER FOR MOMS

Dear Lord, help me break bad habits and form good ones. And let my actions be pleasing to You, today and every day. Amen

The Bible says I should imitate Christ, but I can never be like Him. So what should I do?

THE QUICK ANSWER

While you can't imitate Christ perfectly, you can follow in His footsteps, you can share His Good News, and you can, to the best of your abilities, obey His commandments. And that's what you should do.

Imitating Christ

Therefore, be imitators of God, as dearly loved children.
Ephesians 5:1 HCSB

Imitating Christ is impossible, but attempting to imitate Him is both possible and advisable. By attempting to imitate Jesus, we seek, to the best of our abilities, to walk in His footsteps. To the extent we succeed in following Him, we receive the spiritual abundance that is the rightful possession of those who love Christ and keep His commandments.

Do you seek God's blessings for the day ahead? Then, to the best of your abilities, imitate His Son. You will fall short, of course. But if your heart is right and your intentions are pure, God will bless your efforts, your day, and your life.

Jesus never asks us to give Him what we don't have. But He does demand that we give Him all we do have if we want to be a part of what He wishes to do in the lives of those around us!

Anne Graham Lotz

You cannot cooperate with Jesus in becoming what He wants you to become and simultaneously be what the world desires to make you. If you would say, "Take the world but give me Jesus," then you must deny yourself and take up your cross. The simple truth is that your "self" must be put to death in order for you to get to the point where for you to live is Christ. What will it be? The world and you, or Jesus and you? You do have a choice to make.

Kay Arthur

Every Christian is to become a little Christ. The whole purpose of becoming a Christian is simply nothing else.

C. S. Lewis

A PRAYER FOR MOMS

Dear Lord, You sent Your Son so that I might have abundant life and eternal life. Thank You, Father, for my Savior, Christ Jesus. I will follow Him, honor Him, and share His Good News, this day and every day. Amen

QUESTION 57

Sometimes, life seems so serious. What should our family do about it?

THE QUICK ANSWER

God's Word instructs us to be joyful. As a parent, it's up to you to make certain that your house is a place where everybody can expect to have good clean fun and plenty of laughs.

So Laugh!

There is a time for everything, and everything on earth has its
special season . . . . There is a time to cry and a time to laugh.
There is a time to be sad and a time to dance.

Ecclesiastes 3:1, 4 NCV

Laughter is a gift from God, a gift that He intends for us to use. Yet sometimes, because of the inevitable stresses of everyday living, we fail to find the fun in life. When we allow life's inevitable disappointments to cast a pall over our lives and our souls, we do a profound disservice to ourselves and to our loved ones.

If you've allowed the clouds of life to obscure the blessings of life, perhaps you've formed the unfortunate habit of taking things just a little too seriously. If so, it's time to fret a little less and laugh a little more.

So today, look for the humor that most certainly surrounds you—when you do, you'll find it. And remember: God created laughter for a reason . . . and Father indeed knows best. So laugh!

As you're rushing through life, take time to stop a moment, look into people's eyes, say something kind, and try to make them laugh!

Barbara Johnson

I think everybody ought to be a laughing Christian. I'm convinced that there's just one place where there's not any laughter, and that's hell.

Jerry Clower

A PRAYER FOR MOMS

Dear Lord, laughter is Your gift to me; help me to enjoy it. Today and every day, put a smile on my face, and help me to share that smile with other people, starting with my family. This is the day that You have made, Lord. Let me enjoy it . . . and let me laugh. Amen

I know it's important for everyone in my family to know God. What should we do?

THE QUICK ANSWER

If you and your family members want to gain a more intimate relationship with God, you should study His Word (every day), worship Him (every day), and talk to Him (many times every day).

Getting to Know Him

Knowing God leads to self-control. Self-control leads to patient endurance, and patient endurance leads to godliness.

2 Peter 1:6 NLT

Do you ever wonder if God is really "right here, right now"? Do you wonder if God hears your prayers, if He understands your feelings, or if He really knows your heart? When you have doubts, remember this: God isn't on a coffee break, and He hasn't moved out of town. He's right here, right now, listening to your thoughts and prayers, watching over your every move.

The Bible teaches that a wonderful way to get to know God is simply to be still and listen to Him. But sometimes, you may find it hard to slow down and listen. As the demands of everyday life weigh down upon you, you may be tempted to ignore God's presence or—worse yet—to rebel against His commandments. But, when you quiet yourself and acknowledge His presence, God touches your heart and restores your spirits. So why not let Him do it right now? If you really want to know Him better, silence is a wonderful place to start.

You cannot grow spiritually until you have the assurance that Christ is in your life.

Vonette Bright

Here is our opportunity: we cannot see God, but we can see Christ. Christ was not only the Son of God, but He was the Father. Whatever Christ was, that God is.

Hannah Whitall Smith

It takes all time and eternity to know God.

Oswald Chambers

A PRAYER FOR MOMS

Dear Lord, help me remember the importance of silence. Help me discover quiet moments throughout the day so that I can sense Your presence and Your love. Amen

Sometimes I'm impatient for life to unfold. What does the Bible say about God's timing?

THE QUICK ANSWER

God has very big plans in store for your life, so trust Him and wait patiently for those plans to unfold. And remember: God's timing is best, so don't allow yourself to become discouraged if things don't work out exactly as you wish. Instead of worrying about your future, entrust it to God. He knows exactly what you need and exactly when you need it.

God's Timetable

He has made everything beautiful in its time. He has also set eternity in the hearts of men; yet they cannot fathom what God has done from beginning to end.
Ecclesiastes 3:11 NIV

If you sincerely seek to be a woman of faith, then you must learn to trust God's timing. You will be sorely tempted, however, to do otherwise. Because you are a fallible human being, you are impatient for things to happen. But, God knows better.

God has created a world that unfolds according to His own timetable, not ours . . . thank goodness! We mortals might make a terrible mess of things. God does not.

God's plan does not always happen in the way that we would like or at the time of our own choosing. Our task—as believing Christians who trust in a benevolent, all-knowing Father—is to wait patiently for God to reveal Himself. And reveal Himself He will. Always. But until God's perfect plan is made known, we must walk in faith and never lose hope. And we must continue to trust Him. Always.

He has the right to interrupt your life. He is Lord. When you accepted Him as Lord, you gave Him the right to help Himself to your life anytime He wants.

Henry Blackaby

When there is perplexity there is always guidance—not always at the moment we ask, but in good time, which is God's time. There is no need to fret and stew.

Elisabeth Elliot

A PRAYER FOR MOMS

Lord, my sense of timing is fallible and imperfect; Yours is not. Let me trust in Your timetable for my life, and give me the patience and the wisdom to trust Your plans, not my own. Amen

QUESTION 60

What does the Bible say about listening to God?

THE QUICK ANSWER

Prayer is two-way communication with God. Talking to God isn't enough; you should also listen to Him. Remember: The more often you speak to the Creator, the more often He'll speak to you.

Listening to God

The one who is from God listens to God's words.
This is why you don't listen, because you are not from God.
John 8:47 HCSB

Sometimes God speaks loudly and clearly. More often, He speaks in a quiet voice—and if you are wise, you will be listening carefully when He does. To do so, you must carve out quiet moments each day to study His Word and sense His direction.

Can you quiet yourself long enough to listen to your conscience? Are you attuned to the subtle guidance of your intuition? Are you willing to pray sincerely and then to wait quietly for God's response? Hopefully so. Usually God refrains from sending His messages on stone tablets or city billboards.

More often, He communicates in subtler ways. If you sincerely desire to hear His voice, you must listen carefully, and you must do so in the silent corners of your quiet, willing heart.

God is always listening.

Stormie Omartian

When we come to Jesus stripped of pretensions, with a needy spirit, ready to listen, He meets us at the point of need.

Catherine Marshall

In the soul-searching of our lives, we are to stay quiet so we can hear Him say all that He wants to say to us in our hearts.

Charles Swindoll

A PRAYER FOR MOMS

Heavenly Father, in these quiet moments before this busy day unfolds, I come to You. May my meditations bring You pleasure just as surely as they bring me a clearer sense of Your love and Your peace. May the time I spend in quiet meditation mold my day and my life . . . for You. Amen

It's hard for me to believe in miracles. What assurances can I find in the Bible?

THE QUICK ANSWER

If you're looking for miracles . . . you'll find them. If you're not, you won't.

Do You Believe in Miracles?

With God's power working in us, God can do much,
much more than anything we can ask or imagine.
Ephesians 3:20 NCV

Do you believe that God is at work in the world? And do you also believe that nothing is impossible for Him? If so, then you also believe that God is perfectly capable of doing things that you, as a mere human being with limited vision and limited understanding, would deem to be utterly impossible. And that's precisely what God does.

Since the moment that He created our universe out of nothingness, God has made a habit of doing miraculous things. And He still works miracles today. Expect Him to work miracles in your own life, and then be watchful. With God, absolutely nothing is impossible, including an amazing assortment of miracles that He stands ready, willing, and able to perform for you and yours.

God specializes in things thought impossible.

Catherine Marshall

I could go through this day oblivious to the miracles all around me or I could tune in and "enjoy."

Gloria Gaither

Faith means believing in realities that go beyond sense and sight. It is the awareness of unseen divine realities all around you.

Joni Eareckson Tada

When God is involved, anything can happen. Be open and stay that way. God has a beautiful way of bringing good vibrations out of broken chords.

Charles Swindoll

A PRAYER FOR MOMS

Lord, for You, nothing is impossible. Let me trust in Your power to do the miraculous, and let me trust in Your willingness to work miracles in my life—and in my heart. Amen

QUESTION 62

I'm a busy mom with too many places to be and not enough energy to do everything. What should I do?

THE QUICK ANSWER

Let God help you set priorities that are pleasing to Him. Then, pray for the strength to do the most important things on your to-do list. And finally, insist on getting plenty of sleep, even if it means making the kids turn off the TV earlier than they would prefer.

Energy for Today

Those who hope in the LORD will renew their strength.
They will soar on wings like eagles; they will run
and not grow weary, they will walk and not be faint.
Isaiah 40:31 NIV

If you're a mother with too many demands and too few hours in which to meet them, you are not alone. Motherhood is perhaps the world's most demanding profession. But don't fret: even when it seems that your responsibilities are simply too great to bear, you and God, working together, can handle them. So focus not upon the difficulties of your circumstances, but instead upon God and upon His love for you. Then, ask Him for the strength that you need to fulfill your daily duties.

When you turn your thoughts and prayers to your Heavenly Father, He will give you the energy and the perspective to complete the most important items on your to-do list. And then, once you've done your best, leave the rest up to God. He can handle it . . . and will.

When the dream of our heart is one that God has planted there, a strange happiness flows into us. At that moment, all of the spiritual resources of the universe are released to help us. Our praying is then at one with the will of God and becomes a channel for the Creator's purposes for us and our world.

Catherine Marshall

Worry does not empty tomorrow of its sorrow; it empties today of its strength.

Corrie ten Boom

A PRAYER FOR MOMS

Lord, let me find my strength in You. When I am weary, give me rest. When I feel overwhelmed, let me look to You for my priorities. Let Your power be my power, Lord, and let Your way be my way, today and forever. Amen

Sometimes, I am afraid. What does the Bible say about fear?

THE QUICK ANSWER

If you're feeling fearful or anxious, you must trust God to solve the problems that are simply too big for you to solve.

Beyond Fear

Even when I walk through the dark valley of death,
I will not be afraid, for you are close beside me.
Your rod and your staff protect and comfort me.
Psalm 23:4 NLT

We live in a world that is, at times, a frightening place. We live in a world that is, at times, a discouraging place. We live in a world where life-changing losses can be so painful and so profound that it seems we will never recover. But, with God's help, and with the help of encouraging family members and friends, we can recover.

During the darker days of life, we are wise to remember the words of Jesus, who reassured His disciples, saying, "Take courage! It is I. Don't be afraid" (Matthew 14:27 NIV). Then, with God's comfort and His love in our hearts, we can offer encouragement to others. And by helping them face their fears, we can, in turn, tackle our own problems with courage, determination, and faith.

Worry is a cycle of inefficient thoughts whirling around a center of fear.

Corrie ten Boom

Fear and doubt are conquered by a faith that rejoices. And faith can rejoice because the promises of God are as certain as God Himself.

Kay Arthur

God shields us from most of the things we fear, but when He chooses not to shield us, He unfailingly allots grace in the measure needed.

Elisabeth Elliot

A PRAYER FOR MOMS

Dear Lord, when I am fearful, keep me mindful that You are my protector and my salvation. Thank You, Father, for a perfect love that casts out fear. Because of You, I can live courageously and faithfully this day and every day. Amen

God has given all of my family members special talents and opportunities. How should we use them?

THE QUICK ANSWER

God has given each of you an array of skills and opportunities. If you use your gifts wisely, they're multiplied. If you misuse your gifts—or ignore them altogether—they are lost. God is anxious for you to use your gifts . . . are you?

Using God's Gifts

Each one has his own gift from God,
one in this manner and another in that.
1 Corinthians 7:7 NKJV

Your talents are a gift from God. And, the same applies to your children. Their talents, too, are blessings from the Creator, blessings which must be nurtured or forfeited.

Are you and your loved ones willing to use your gifts in the way that God intends? Are you willing to summon the discipline that is required to develop your talents and to hone your skills? That's precisely what God wants you to do, and that's precisely what you should desire for yourselves.

So be faithful stewards of your talents and treasures. And then prepare yourselves for even greater blessings that are sure to come.

Not everyone possesses boundless energy or a conspicuous talent. We are not equally blessed with great intellect or physical beauty or emotional strength. But we have all been given the same ability to be faithful.

Gigi Graham Tchividjian

The Lord has abundantly blessed me all of my life. I'm not trying to pay Him back for all of His wonderful gifts; I just realize that He gave them to me to give away.

Lisa Whelchel

One thing taught large in the Holy Scriptures is that while God gives His gifts freely, He will require a strict accounting of them at the end of the road. Each man is personally responsible for his store, be it large or small, and will be required to explain his use of it before the judgment seat of Christ.

A. W. Tozer

A PRAYER FOR MOMS

Lord, I praise You for Your priceless gifts. I give thanks for Your creation, for Your Son, and for the unique talents and opportunities that You have given me. Let me use my gifts for the glory of Your kingdom, this day and every day. Amen

What does the Bible say about optimism?

THE QUICK ANSWER

The Bible promises that if you've given your heart to Jesus, your eternal future is secure. So even when times are tough, you can be hopeful, joyful, and optimistic.

Share Your Optimism

My cup runs over. Surely goodness and mercy shall follow me all the days of my life; and I will dwell in the house of the Lord Forever.
Psalm 23:5-6 NKJV

Because you are a conscientious mom living in a difficult world, you may find yourself pulled down by the inevitable demands and worries of everyday life in the 21st century. Ours is a world brimming with temptations, distractions, and dangers. Sometimes, we can't help ourselves: we worry for our families, and we worry for ourselves.

If you become discouraged, exhausted, or both, then it's time to take your concerns to God. Whether you find yourself at the pinnacle of the mountain or the darkest depths of the valley, God is there. Open your heart to Him and He will lift your spirits and renew your strength.

Today, as a gift to your family and yourself, why not claim the joy that is rightfully yours in Christ? Why not take time to celebrate God's glorious creation? Why not trust your hopes instead of your fears? When you do, you will think optimistically about yourself and your world . . . and you can then share your optimism with others. They'll be better for it, and so will you. But not necessarily in that order.

Make the least of all that goes and the most of all that comes. Don't regret what is past. Cherish what you have. Look forward to all that is to come. And most important of all, rely moment by moment on Jesus Christ.

Gigi Graham Tchividjian

We may run, walk, stumble, drive, or fly, but let us never lose sight of the reason for the journey, or miss a chance to see a rainbow on the way.

Gloria Gaither

A PRAYER FOR MOMS

Dear Lord, I will look for the best in other people, I will expect the best from You, and I will try my best to do my best—today and every day. Amen

QUESTION 66

It's easy for me to focus on the past. What should I do?

THE QUICK ANSWER

Remember that the past is past. So focus on the opportunities ahead of you, not the disappointments behind you.

Making Peace with the Past

Do not remember the past events, pay no attention to things of old.
Look, I am about to do something new; even now it is coming.
Do you not see it? Indeed, I will make a way
in the wilderness, rivers in the desert.
Isaiah 43:18-19 HCSB

Have you made peace with your past? If so, congratulations. But, if you are mired in the quicksand of regret, it's time to plan your escape. How can you do so? By accepting what has been and by trusting God for what will be.

Because you are human, you may be slow to forget yesterday's disappointments; if so you are not alone. But if you sincerely seek to focus your hopes and energies on the future, then you must find ways to accept the past, no matter how difficult it may be to do so.

If you have not yet made peace with the past, today is the day to declare an end to all hostilities. When you do, you can then turn your thoughts to the wondrous promises of God and to the glorious future that He has in store for you.

Shake the dust from your past, and move forward in His promises.

Kay Arthur

Whoever you are, whatever your condition or circumstance, whatever your past or problem, Jesus can restore you to wholeness.

Anne Graham Lotz

Yesterday is just experience but tomorrow is glistening with purpose—and today is the channel leading from one to the other.

Barbara Johnson

A PRAYER FOR MOMS

Heavenly Father, free me from anger, resentment, and envy. When I am bitter, I cannot feel the peace that You intend for my life. Keep me mindful that forgiveness is Your commandment, and help me accept the past, treasure the present, and trust the future . . . to You. Amen

Sometimes I'm worried about the future. What does God's Word say about my future?

THE QUICK ANSWER

If you've given your heart to Jesus, God's Word promises that your future is intensely bright. Of course, you and your loved ones may encounter adversity and pain, but your eternal destiny is secure.

Your Bright Future

"I say this because I know what I am planning for you,"
says the Lord. "I have good plans for you, not plans to hurt you.
I will give you hope and a good future."
Jeremiah 29:11 NCV

Because we are saved by a risen Christ, we can have hope for the future, no matter how troublesome our present circumstances may seem. Of course, we will face disappointments and failures while we are here on earth, but these are only temporary defeats. Of course, this world can be a place of trials and tribulations, but when we place our trust in the Giver of all things good, we are secure. God has promised us peace, joy, and eternal life. And God keeps His promises today, tomorrow, and forever.

Are you willing to place your future in the hands of a loving and all-knowing God? Do you trust in the ultimate goodness of His plan for your life? Will you face today's challenges with optimism and hope? You should. After all, God created you for a very important purpose: His purpose. And you still have important work to do: His work.

Today, as you live in the present and look to the future, remember that God has a plan for you. Act—and believe—accordingly.

Joy comes from knowing God loves me and knows who I am and where I'm going . . . that my future is secure as I rest in Him.

James Dobson

The future lies all before us. Shall it only be a slight advance upon what we usually do? Ought it not to be a bound, a leap forward to altitudes of endeavor and success undreamed of before?

Annie Armstrong

A PRAYER FOR MOMS

Dear Lord, as I look to the future, I will place my trust in You. If I become discouraged, I will turn to You. If I am afraid, I will seek strength in You. You are my Father, and I will place my hope, my trust, and my faith in You. Amen

QUESTION 68

We live in a noisy world where it's hard to find a moment's peace. What does the Bible teach us about peace?

THE QUICK ANSWER

God's peace surpasses human understanding. When you accept His peace, it will revolutionize your life.

Sharing His Peace

And the peace of God, which surpasses all comprehension, will guard your hearts and your minds in Christ Jesus.
Philippians 4:7 NASB

The beautiful words of John 14:27 give us hope: "Peace I leave with you, my peace I give unto you . . . ." Jesus offers us peace, not as the world gives, but as He alone gives. We, as believers, can accept His peace or ignore it.

When we accept the peace of Jesus Christ into our hearts, our lives are transformed. And then, because we possess the gift of peace, we can share that gift with fellow Christians, family members, friends, and associates. If, on the other hand, we choose to ignore the gift of peace—for whatever reason—we cannot share what we do not possess.

As every young woman knows, peace can be a scarce commodity in a demanding, 21st-century world. How, then, can we find the peace that we so desperately desire? By turning our days and our lives over to God. Elisabeth Elliot writes, "If my life is surrendered to God, all is well. Let me not grab it back, as though it were in peril in His hand but would be safer in mine!" May we give our lives, our hopes, and our prayers to the Lord, and, by doing so, accept His will and His peace.

The fruit of our placing all things in God's hands is the presence of His abiding peace in our hearts.

Hannah Whitall Smith

God's peace is like a river, not a pond. In other words, a sense of health and well-being, both of which are expressions of the Hebrew shalom, can permeate our homes even when we're in white-water rapids.

Beth Moore

When we do what is right, we have contentment, peace, and happiness.

Beverly LaHaye

A PRAYER FOR MOMS

Dear Lord, I will open my heart to You. And I thank You, God, for Your love, for Your peace, and for Your Son. Amen

What does the Bible say about my children?

THE QUICK ANSWER

The Bible states that your children are a gift from God—a gift that should be treasured and nurtured.

Your Children: A Treasure from God

Children are a gift from the LORD; they are a reward from him.

Psalm 127:4 NLT

As a mother, you are keenly aware that God has entrusted you with a priceless treasure from above: your child. Every child is different, yet every child is similar in this respect: every child is a glorious gift from above—and with that gift comes immense responsibilities.

Thoughtful mothers (like you) understand the critical importance of raising their children with love, with family, with discipline, and with God. By making God a focus in the home, loving mothers offer a priceless legacy to their children—a legacy of hope, a legacy of love, a legacy of wisdom.

Today, let us pray for our children . . . all of them. Let us pray for our own children and for children around the world.

Every child is God's child. May we, as concerned mothers, behave—and pray—accordingly.

Children are not so different from kites. Children were created to fly. But, they need wind, the undergirding, and strength that comes from unconditional love, encouragement, and prayer.

Gigi Graham Tchividjian

Our faithfulness, or lack of it, will have an overwhelming impact on the heritage of our children.

Beth Moore

When Jesus put the little child in the midst of His disciples, He did not tell the little child to become like His disciples; He told the disciples to become like the little child.

Ruth Bell Graham

A PRAYER FOR MOMS

Lord, You have given me a wonderful responsibility: caring for my children. Let me love them, care for them, nurture them, teach them, and lead them to You. When I am weary, give me strength. When I am frustrated, give me patience. And, let my words and deeds always demonstrate to my children the love that I feel for them . . . and for You. Amen

QUESTION 70

How should I respond to Jesus' sacrifice on the cross?

THE QUICK ANSWER

Jesus made an incredible sacrifice for you. Now, it's your turn to respond to Christ's sacrifice by turning your heart and your soul over to Him.

Considering the Cross

But as for me, I will never boast about anything except the cross of our Lord Jesus Christ, through whom the world has been crucified to me, and I to the world.
Galatians 6:14 HCSB

As we consider Christ's sacrifice on the cross, we should be profoundly humbled and profoundly grateful. And today, as we come to Christ in prayer, we should do so in a spirit of quiet, heartfelt devotion to the One who gave His life so that we might have life eternal.

He was the Son of God, but He wore a crown of thorns. He was the Savior of mankind, yet He was put to death on a rough-hewn cross made of wood. He offered His healing touch to an unsaved world, and yet the same hands that had healed the sick and raised the dead were pierced with nails.

Christ humbled Himself on a cross—for you. He shed His blood—for you. He has offered to walk with you through this life and throughout all eternity. As you approach Him today in prayer, think about His sacrifice and His grace. And be humble.

Jesus challenges you and me to keep our focus daily on the cross of His will if we want to be His disciples.

Anne Graham Lotz

God is my Heavenly Father. He loves me with an everlasting love. The proof of that is the Cross.

Elisabeth Elliot

The cross takes care of the past. The cross takes care of the flesh. The cross takes care of the world.

Kay Arthur

A PRAYER FOR MOMS

Dear Jesus, You are my Savior and my protector. You suffered on the cross for me, and I will give You honor and praise every day of my life. I will honor You with my words, my thoughts, and my prayers. And I will live according to Your commandments, so that thorough me, others might come to know Your perfect love. Amen

When I displease God or injure other people, what can I do? How can I make things right with God?

THE QUICK ANSWER

If you're engaged in behavior that is displeasing to God, today is the day to stop. First, confess your sins to God. Then, ask Him what actions you should take in order to make things right again.

Real Repentance

Come back to the LORD and live!
Amos 5:6 NLT

Who among us has sinned? All of us. But, God calls upon us to turn away from sin by following His commandments. And the good news is this: When we do ask God's forgiveness and turn our hearts to Him, He forgives us absolutely and completely.

Genuine repentance requires more than simply offering God apologies for our misdeeds. Real repentance may start with feelings of sorrow and remorse, but it ends only when we turn away from the sin that has heretofore distanced us from our Creator. In truth, we offer our most meaningful apologies to God, not with our words, but with our actions. As long as we are still engaged in sin, we may be "repenting," but we have not fully "repented."

Is there an aspect of your life that is distancing you from God? If so, ask for His forgiveness, and—just as importantly—stop sinning. Then, wrap yourself in the protection of God's Word. When you do, you will be secure.

When true repentance comes, God will not hesitate for a moment to forgive, cast the sins in the sea of forgetfulness, and put the child on the road to restoration.

Beth Moore

Four marks of true repentance are: acknowledgement of wrong, willingness to confess it, willingness to abandon it, and willingness to make restitution.

Corrie ten Boom

A PRAYER FOR MOMS

When I stray from Your commandments, Lord, I must not only confess my sins, I must also turn from them. When I fall short, help me to change. When I reject Your Word and Your will for my life, guide me back to Your side. Forgive my sins, Dear Lord, and help me live according to Your plan for my life. Your plan is perfect, Father; I am not. Let me trust in You. Amen

What does the Bible say about sadness and sorrow?

THE QUICK ANSWER

The thought of a sovereign and loving God will help dispel the inevitable sadness you'll experience from time to time.

On Sad Days

Why am I so depressed? Why this turmoil within me?
Put your hope in God, for I will still praise Him,
my Savior and my God.
Psalm 42:11 HCSB

Some days are light and happy, and some days are not. When we face the inevitable dark days of life, we must choose how we will respond. Will we allow ourselves to sink even more deeply into our own sadness, or will we do the difficult work of pulling ourselves out?

We bring light to the dark days of life by turning first to God, and then to trusted family members and friends. Then, we must go to work solving the problems that confront us. When we do, the clouds will eventually part, and the sun will shine once more upon our souls.

The strengthening of faith comes from staying with it in the hour of trial. We should not shrink from tests of faith.

Catherine Marshall

God is good, and heaven is forever. These two facts should brighten up even the darkest day.

Marie T. Freeman

When life is difficult, God wants us to have a faith that trusts and waits.

Kay Arthur

When we cry, we allow our bodies to function according to God's design—and we embrace one of the "perks" he offers to relieve our stress.

Barbara Johnson

A PRAYER FOR MOMS

Dear Heavenly Father, on those days when I am troubled, You comfort me if I turn my thoughts and prayers to You. When I am afraid, You protect me. When I am discouraged, You lift me up. You are my unending source of strength, Lord. In every circumstance, let me trust Your plan and Your will for my life. Amen

QUESTION 73

How does the Bible describe God?

THE QUICK ANSWER

Of course we mortals can never begin to understand or comprehend the Creator. But the Bible teaches us this much: God is love. And we should find comfort in that fact.

God Is Love

God is love, and the one who remains in love remains in God, and God remains in him.

1 John 4:16 HCSB

The Bible makes this promise: God is love. It's a sweeping statement, a profoundly important description of what God is and how God works. God's love is perfect. When we open our hearts to His perfect love, we are touched by the Creator's hand, and we are transformed.

Today, even if you can only carve out a few quiet moments, offer sincere prayers of thanksgiving to your Creator. He loves you now and throughout all eternity. Open your heart to His presence and His love.

Let God have you, and let God love you—and don't be surprised if your heart begins to hear music you've never heard and your feet learn to dance as never before.

Max Lucado

I can tell you, from personal experience of walking with God for over fifty years, that He is the Lover of my soul.

Vonette Bright

...God loves these people too, just because they're unattractive or warped in their thinking doesn't mean the Lord doesn't love them.

Ruth Bell Graham

As God's children, we are the recipients of lavish love—a love that motivates us to keep trusting even when we have no idea what God is doing.

Beth Moore

A PRAYER FOR MOMS

Dear Lord, the Bible tells me that You are my loving Father. I thank You, Lord, for Your love and for Your Son. Amen

Sometimes it's hard to be an obedient Christian. What does the Bible say about obedience?

THE QUICK ANSWER

God rewards obedience and punishes disobedience. It's not enough to understand God's rules; you must also live by them or face the consequences.

Obedience Now

For God is working in you, giving you the desire to obey him and the power to do what pleases him.
Philippians 2:13 NLT

As loving parents, we must teach our children to obey the rules of society and the laws of God. God's laws are contained in a guidebook for righteous living called the Holy Bible. It contains thorough instructions which, if followed, lead to fulfillment, peace, righteousness, and salvation. But, if we choose to ignore God's commandments, the results are as predictable as they are tragic.

Talking about obedience is easy; living obediently is considerably harder. But, if we are to be responsible role models for our families and friends, we must study God's Word and obey it.

Phillips Brooks advised, "Be such a person, and live such a life, that if every person were such as you, and every life a life like yours, this earth would be God's Paradise." And that's sound advice because our families and friends are watching . . . and so, for that matter, is God.

God is God. Because He is God, He is worthy of my trust and obedience. I will find rest nowhere but in His holy will, a will that is unspeakably beyond my largest notions of what He is up to.

Elisabeth Elliot

The pathway of obedience can sometimes be difficult, but it always leads to a strengthening of our inner woman.

Vonette Bright

A PRAYER FOR MOMS

Dear Lord, make me a mother who is obedient to Your Word. Let me live according to Your commandments. Direct my path far from the temptations and distractions of this world. And, let me discover Your will and follow it, Lord, this day and always. Amen

What does the Bible say about mentors?

THE QUICK ANSWER

God's Word instructs us to rely on the advice of trusted friends and mentors. Proverbs 1:5 makes it clear: "A wise man will hear and increase learning, and a man of understanding will attain wise counsel" (NKJV).

Walking with the Wise

Listen to advice and accept correction,
and in the end you will be wise.
Proverbs 19:20 NCV

Do you wish to become wise? Then you must walk with people who, by their words and their presence, make you wiser. And, to the best of your ability, you must avoid those people who encourage you to think foolish thoughts or do foolish things.

Today, as a gift to yourself, select, from your friends and family members, a mentor whose judgement you trust. Then listen carefully to your mentor's advice and be willing to accept that advice, even if accepting it requires effort or pain, or both. Consider your mentor to be God's gift to you. Thank God for that gift, and use it.

The next best thing to being wise oneself is to live in a circle of those who are.

C. S. Lewis

It takes a wise person to give good advice, but an even wiser person to take it.

Marie T. Freeman

No matter how crazy or nutty your life has seemed, God can make something strong and good out of it. He can help you grow wide branches for others to use as shelter.

Barbara Johnson

Yes, the Spirit was sent to be our Counselor. Yes, Jesus speaks to us personally. But often he works through another human being.

John Eldredge

A PRAYER FOR MOMS

Dear Lord, thank You for family members, for friends, and for mentors. When I am troubled, let me turn to them for help, for guidance, for comfort, and for perspective. And Father, let me be a friend and mentor to others, so that my love for You may be reflected in my genuine concern for them. Amen

Sundays have become very busy around our house. Our schedules are full, and we hardly have time to slow down long enough to catch our breath. In the future, how should we reorganize our Sundays?

THE QUICK ANSWER

The world considers Sunday to be just another day—but you shouldn't fall prey to that sort of thinking. As a Christian parent, it's up to you to decide how your family will spend Sundays. Please decide wisely.

Observing the Sabbath

Remember the Sabbath day, to keep it holy.
Exodus 20:8 NKJV

When God gave Moses the Ten Commandments, it became perfectly clear that our Heavenly Father intends for us to make the Sabbath a holy day, a day for worship, for contemplation, for fellowship, and for rest. Yet we live in a seven-day-a-week world, a world that all too often treats Sunday as a regular workday.

How does your family observe the Lord's day? When church is over, do you treat Sunday like any other day of the week? If so, it's time to think long and hard about your family's schedule and your family's priorities.

Whenever we ignore God's commandments, we pay a price. So if you've been treating Sunday as just another day, it's time to break that habit. When Sunday rolls around, don't try to fill every spare moment. Take time to rest . . . Father's orders!

God asks that we worship Him with our concentrated minds as well as with our wills and emotions. A divided and scattered mind is not effective.

Catherine Marshall

God has promised to give you all of eternity. The least you can do is give Him one day a week in return.

Marie T. Freeman

It's our privilege to not only raise our hands in worship but also to combine the visible with the invisible in a rising stream of praise and adoration sent directly to our Father.

Shirley Dobson

A PRAYER FOR MOMS

Dear Lord, I thank You for the Sabbath day, a day when my family and I can worship You and praise Your Son. We will keep the Sabbath as a holy day, a day when we can honor You. Amen

Sometimes, it's easy to think, "I've done that," when it was, in truth, God who did it. So what does the Bible say about humility?

THE QUICK ANSWER

God favors the humble just as surely as He disciplines the proud. So you must remain humble or face the consequences. Pride does go before the fall, but humility often prevents the fall.

The Beauty of Humility

For everyone who exalts himself will be humbled,
and the one who humbles himself will be exalted.
Luke 14:11 HCSB

Humility is not, in most cases, a naturally occurring human trait. Most of us, it seems, are more than willing to overestimate our own accomplishments. We are tempted to say, "Look how wonderful I am!" . . . hoping all the while that the world will agree with our own self-appraisals.

God honors humility . . . and He rewards those who humbly serve Him. When we acquire the wisdom to be humble, we bring enlightenment to the world (and blessings to ourselves).

But if we cannot overcome the tendency to overestimate our own accomplishments, then God still has some important lessons to teach us—lessons about the wisdom, the power, and the beauty of humility.

If you know who you are in Christ, your personal ego is not an issue.

Beth Moore

Humility is the fairest and rarest flower that blooms.

Charles Swindoll

That some of my hymns have been dictated by the blessed Holy Spirit I have no doubt; and that others have been the result of deep meditation I know to be true; but that the poet has any right to claim special merit for himself is certainly presumptuous.

Fanny Crosby

A PRAYER FOR MOMS

Lord, You are great, and I am human. Keep me humble, and keep me mindful that all my gifts come from You. Amen

I try to do my best, but sometimes, despite my best efforts, I make big mistakes. What does the Bible say about that?

THE QUICK ANSWER

Time and again, the Bible preaches the power of perseverance. Setbacks, disappointments, and failures are inevitable—your response to them is optional. If you don't give up, you can turn your stumbling blocks into stepping stones . . . and you should.

Beyond Failure

Even though good people may be bothered by trouble seven times, they are never defeated.
Proverbs 24:16 NCV

The occasional disappointments and failures of life are inevitable. Such setbacks are simply the price that we must occasionally pay for our willingness to take risks as we follow our dreams. But even when we encounter bitter disappointments, we must never lose faith.

As parents, we are far from perfect. And, without question, our children are imperfect as well. When we make mistakes, we must correct them and learn from them. And, when our children make mistakes, we must help them do likewise.

In essence, my testimony is that there is life after failure: abundant, effective, spirit-filled life for those who are willing to repent hard and work hard.

Beth Moore

The difference between winning and losing is how we choose to react to disappointment.

Barbara Johnson

One of the ways God refills us after failure is through the blessing of Christian fellowship. Just experiencing the joy of simple activities shared with other children of God can have a healing effect on us.

Anne Graham Lotz

How beautiful it is to learn that grace isn't fragile, and that in the family of God we can fail and not be a failure.

Gloria Gaither

A PRAYER FOR MOMS

Dear Lord, when I encounter failures and disappointments, keep me mindful that You are in control. Let me persevere—even if my soul is troubled—and let me follow Your Son, Jesus Christ, this day and forever. Amen

QUESTION 79

How best can I teach my children the importance of self-discipline?

THE QUICK ANSWER

If you want to teach discipline, you must be disciplined in your own approach to life. You can't teach it if you won't live it.

The Rewards of Discipline

God hasn't invited us into a disorderly, unkempt life but into something holy and beautiful—as beautiful on the inside as the outside.
1 Thessalonians 4:7 MSG

Wise mothers teach their children the importance of discipline using their words and their examples. Disciplined moms understand that God doesn't reward laziness or misbehavior. To the contrary, God expects His believers to lead lives that are above reproach. And, He punishes those who disobey His commandments.

It has been said that there are no shortcuts to any place worth going. Thoughtful mothers agree. In Proverbs 28:19,

God's message is clear: "He who works his land will have abundant food, but the one who chases fantasies will have his fill of poverty" (NIV).

When we work diligently and consistently, we can expect a bountiful harvest. But we must never expect the harvest to precede the labor. First, we must lead lives of discipline and obedience; then, we will reap the never-ending rewards that God has promised.

If you want a surefire way to reshape the future, here it is: find something important to say to the next generation . . . and say it.

Marie T. Freeman

Train your child in the way in which you know you should have gone yourself.

C. H. Spurgeon

A PRAYER FOR MOMS

Lord, let me be a disciplined parent, and let me teach my children to lead disciplined lives. Let me be Your faithful servant and let me teach faithfulness by my walk and by my talk. Let me raise my family in the knowledge of Your Word, and let me follow Your commandments just as surely as I teach my children to obey You and to love You. Amen

QUESTION 80

What does the Bible have to say about happiness?

THE QUICK ANSWER

Jesus intends for our joy to be complete (John 15:11). And He came to earth so that we might experience His abundance (John 10:10). So, if we're wise, we'll open our hearts to Christ and celebrate His gifts today, tomorrow, and forever.

Happiness Now

But happy are those . . . whose hope is in the LORD their God.
Psalm 146:5 NLT

Okay, Mom, it's been a typical day. You've cared for your family, worked your fingers to the bone, rushed from Point A to Point Z, and taken barely a moment for yourself. But have you taken time to smile? If so, you're a very wise woman. If not, it's time to slow down, to take a deep breath, and to recount your blessings!

God has promised all of us the opportunity to experience spiritual abundance and peace. But it's up to each of us to claim the spiritual riches that God has in store. God promises us a life of fulfillment and joy, but He does not force His joy upon us.

Would you like to experience the peace and the joy that God intends for you? Then accept His Son and lay claim to His promises. And then, put a smile on your face that stretches all the way down to your heart. When you do, you'll discover that when you smile at God, He smiles back.

Christ is the secret, the source, the substance, the center, and the circumference of all true and lasting gladness.

Mrs. Charles E. Cowman

I became aware of one very important concept I had missed before: my attitude—not my circumstances—was what was making me unhappy.

Vonette Bright

When we bring sunshine into the lives of others, we're warmed by it ourselves. When we spill a little happiness, it splashes on us.

Barbara Johnson

A PRAYER FOR MOMS

Lord, let me be a mother who celebrates life. Let me rejoice in the gift of this day, and let me praise You for the gift of Your Son. Let me be a joyful Christian, Lord, as I share Your Good News with friends, with family, and with the world. Amen

QUESTION 81

When I look in the mirror, I'm not crazy about what I see. What does the Bible have to say about age and beauty?

THE QUICK ANSWER

The Bible teaches us that genuine beauty is inner beauty.

Age and Beauty

Your beauty should not be the outer beauty of elaborate hairstyles and the wearing of gold ornaments or of fine clothes; rather, it should be an inner beauty with the imperishability of a gentle and quiet spirit, which is very valuable in God's eyes.
1 Peter 3:3-4 HCSB

We live in a society that glorifies youth. The messages that we receive from the media are unrelenting: We are told that we must do everything within our power to retain youthful values and a youthful appearance. The goal, we are told, is to remain "forever young"—yet this goal is not only unrealistic; it is also unworthy of women who understand what genuine beauty is, and what it isn't. When it comes to "health and beauty" . . . you should focus more on health than on beauty. In fact, when you take care of your physical, spiritual, and mental health, your appearance will tend to take care of itself. And remember: God loves you during every stage of life—so embrace the aging process for what it is: an opportunity to grow closer to your loved ones and to your Creator.

No matter how old they grow, some people never lose their beauty. They merely move it from their faces into their hearts.

Barbara Johnson

Don't talk of growing old. If you continually talk of it, you may bring it on.

Hannah Whitall Smith

Youth and age touch only the surface of our lives.

C. S. Lewis

A PRAYER FOR MOMS

Dear Lord, through every stage of life, I will praise You for Your blessings, for Your love, and for Your Son. Let me be a joyful believer every day of my life. Amen

What does the Bible say about the search for purpose and meaning?

THE QUICK ANSWER

God has a wonderful plan for you and your family. Discovering God's purpose requires a willingness to be open. God's plan is unfolding day by day. If you keep your eyes and your heart open, He'll reveal His plans. God has big things in store for you, but He may have quite a few lessons to teach you before you are fully prepared to do His will and fulfill His purposes.

A Mother's Mission

Commit your activities to the Lord and your plans will be achieved.
Proverbs 16:3 HCSB

Whether you realize it or not, you are on a personal mission for God. As a Christian mother, that mission is straightforward: Honor God, accept Christ as your Savior, raise your children in a loving, Christ-centered home, and be a servant to those who cross your path.

Of course, you will encounter impediments as you attempt to discover the exact nature of God's purpose for your life, but you must never lose sight of the overriding purposes that God has established for all believers. You will encounter these overriding purposes again and again as you worship your Creator and study His Word.

Every day offers countless opportunities to serve God and to worship Him. When you do so, He will bless you in miraculous ways. May you continue to seek God's will, may you trust His Word, and may you place Him where He belongs: at the very center of your life.

His life is our light—our purpose and meaning and reason for living.

Anne Graham Lotz

In the very place where God has put us, whatever its limitations, whatever kind of work it may be, we may indeed serve the Lord Christ.

Elisabeth Elliot

A PRAYER FOR MOMS

Dear Lord, let Your purposes be my purposes. Let Your priorities be my priorities. Let Your will be my will. Let Your Word be my guide. And, let me grow in faith and in wisdom today and every day. Amen

So many people around me seem to need encouragement. What should I do?

THE QUICK ANSWER

Do you want to be successful and go far in life? Encourage others to do the same. You can't lift other people up without lifting yourself up, too. And remember the words of Oswald Chambers: "God grant that we may not hinder those who are battling their way slowly into the light."

The Gift of Encouragement

Let's see how inventive we can be in encouraging love and helping out, not avoiding worshipping together as some do but spurring each other on.
Hebrews 10:24-25 MSG

Your loved ones need a regular supply of encouraging words and pats on the back. And you need the rewards that God gives to enthusiastic moms who are a continual source of encouragement to their families.

The 118th Psalm reminds us, "This is the day which the Lord hath made; we will rejoice and be glad in it" (v. 24 KJV).

As we rejoice in this day that the Lord has given us, let us remember that an important part of today's celebration is the time we spend celebrating others. Each day provides countless opportunities to encourage others and to praise their good works. When we do, we not only spread seeds of joy and happiness, we also follow the commandments of God's Holy Word.

Today, look for the good in others—starting with your loved ones. And then, celebrate the good that you find. When you do, you'll be a powerful force of encouragement in your corner of the world . . . and a worthy servant to your God.

The glory of friendship is not the outstretched hand, or the kindly smile, or the joy of companionship. It is the spiritual inspiration that comes to one when he discovers that someone else believes in him and is willing to trust him with his friendship.

Corrie ten Boom

A PRAYER FOR MOMS

Dear Lord, help me be a thoughtful mother and a genuine source of encouragement to my family. Just as You have lifted me up, let me also lift up my loved ones with a spirit of enthusiasm and hope. Amen

The Bible makes many promises. Can I depend upon those promises?

THE QUICK ANSWER

Yes! God is always faithful and His Word endures forever. So you and your family should study God's Word (every day) and trust it. When you do, you will be blessed.

God's Promises

Patient endurance is what you need now, so you will continue to do God's will. Then you will receive all that he has promised.
Hebrews 10:36 NLT

The Bible contains promises, made by God, upon which we, as believers, can and must depend. But sometimes, especially when we find ourselves caught in the inevitable entanglements of life, we fail to trust God completely.

Are you tired? Discouraged? Fearful? Be comforted and trust the promises that God has made to you. Are you worried or anxious? Be confident in God's power. Do you see a difficult future ahead? Be courageous and call upon God. He will protect you and then use you according to His purposes. Are you confused? Listen to the quiet voice of your Heavenly Father.

He is not a God of confusion. Talk with Him; listen to Him; trust Him, and trust His promises. He is steadfast, and He is your Protector . . . forever.

Shake the dust from your past, and move forward in His promises.

Kay Arthur

We have ample evidence that the Lord is able to guide. The promises cover every imaginable situation. All we need to do is to take the hand he stretches out.

Elisabeth Elliot

Claim all of God's promises in the Bible. Your sins, your worries, your life—you may cast them all on Him.

Corrie ten Boom

A PRAYER FOR MOMS

Lord, Your Holy Word contains promises, and I will trust them. I will use the Bible as my guide, and I will trust You, Lord, to speak to me through Your Holy Spirit and through Your Holy Word, this day and forever. Amen

As a busy mom, my world seems filled with distractions. How can I focus more intently on the things that really matter?

THE QUICK ANSWER

Have a daily devotional every morning, keep praying throughout the day, and don't support any activity that distances you from God's path or from your most important priorities. Put first things first, starting with God.

Too Many Distractions?

*Let us lay aside every weight and the sin that so easily ensnares us,
and run with endurance the race that lies before us,
keeping our eyes on Jesus, the source and perfecter of our faith.*
Hebrews 12:1-2 HCSB

All of us must live through those days when the traffic jams, the computer crashes, and the dog makes a main course out of our homework. But, when we find ourselves distracted by the minor frustrations of life, we must catch ourselves, take a deep breath, and lift our thoughts upward.

Although we may, at times, struggle mightily to rise above the distractions of everyday living, we need never struggle alone. God is here—eternal and faithful, with infinite patience and love—and, if we reach out to Him, He will restore our sense of perspective and give peace to our souls.

Setting goals is one way you can be sure that you will focus your efforts on the main things so that trivial matters will not become your focus.

Charles Stanley

When Jesus is in our midst, He brings His limitless power along as well. But, Jesus must be in the middle, all eyes and hearts focused on Him.

Shirley Dobson

We need to stop focusing on our lacks and stop giving out excuses and start looking at and listening to Jesus.

Anne Graham Lotz

There is an enormous power in little things to distract our attention from God.

Oswald Chambers

A PRAYER FOR MOMS

Dear Lord, help me to face this day with a spirit of optimism and thanksgiving. And let me focus my thoughts on You and Your incomparable gifts. Amen

How does God want me to love my family?

THE QUICK ANSWER

A mother's love must always be demonstrated with deeds, not just announced with words. You demonstrate your love by giving of yourself and your time, no matter how busy you are. Be sure to watch your youngster carefully and listen with your ears, your eyes, and your heart. And remember: wise moms pay careful attention to the things their children don't say.

A Mother's Love

Her children rise up and call her blessed.
Proverbs 31:28 NKJV

Few things in life are as precious or as enduring as a mother's love. Our mothers give us life, and they care for us. They nurture us when we are sick and encourage us when we're brokenhearted. Indeed, a mother's love is both powerful and priceless.

The words of 1st Corinthians 13 remind us that faith is important; so, too, is hope. But love is more important still. Christ showed His love for us on the cross, and, as Christians, we are called upon to return Christ's love by sharing it. Sometimes love is easy (puppies and sleeping children come to mind) and sometimes love is hard (fallible human beings come to mind). But God's Word is clear: We are to love our families and our neighbors without reservation or condition.

As a caring mother, you are not only shaping the lives of your loved ones; you are also, in a very real sense, reshaping eternity. It's a big job, a job so big, in fact, that God saw fit to entrust it to some of the most important people in His kingdom: loving moms like you.

As a mother, my job is to take care of the possible and trust God with the impossible.

Ruth Bell Graham

The mother is and must be, whether she knows it or not, the greatest, strongest, and most lasting teacher her children have.

Hannah Whitall Smith

A PRAYER FOR MOMS

Dear Lord, Your love for me endures forever; so, too, does my love for my own children. Help me to use my role as a mother, Lord, to lavish love upon these precious souls You have placed in my care. Amen

As a Christian parent, when should I expect to receive God's abundance?

THE QUICK ANSWER

God's abundance is available to you right here, right now. And it's up to you to claim it.

God's Abundance

I came that they may have life, and have it abundantly.

John 10:10 NASB

Are you the kind of mom who accepts God's spiritual abundance without reservation? If so, you are availing yourself of the peace and the joy that He has promised. Do you sincerely seek the riches that our Savior offers to those who give themselves to Him? Then follow Him. When you do, you will receive the love and the abundance that Jesus offers to those who follow Him.

Seek first the salvation that is available through a personal, passionate relationship with Christ, and then claim the joy, the peace, and the spiritual abundance that the Shepherd offers His sheep.

If we were given all we wanted here, our hearts would settle for this world rather than the next.

Elisabeth Elliot

Jesus intended for us to be overwhelmed by the blessings of regular days. He said it was the reason he had come: "I am come that they might have life, and that they might have it more abundantly."

Gloria Gaither

God is the giver, and we are the receivers. And His richest gifts are bestowed not upon those who do the greatest things, but upon those who accept His abundance and His grace.

Hannah Whitall Smith

The gift of God is eternal life, spiritual life, abundant life through faith in Jesus Christ, the Living Word of God.

Anne Graham Lotz

A PRAYER FOR MOMS

Dear Lord, You have offered me the gift of abundance through Your Son. Thank You, Father, for the abundant life that is mine through Christ Jesus. Let me accept His gifts and use them always to glorify You. Amen

When I'm overcome by worries, what should I do . . . and where should I turn?

THE QUICK ANSWER

Carefully divide your areas of concern into two categories: those things you can control and those you cannot control. Once you've done so, spend your time working to resolve the things you can control, and entrust everything else to God.

Beyond Worry

Let not your heart be troubled; you believe in God, believe also in Me.
John 14:1 NKJV

If you are like most mothers, it is simply a fact of life: from time to time, you worry. You worry about children, about health, about finances, about safety, and about countless other challenges of life, some great and some small. Where is the best place to take your worries? Take them to God. Take your troubles to Him, and your fears and your sorrows.

Barbara Johnson correctly observed, "Worry is the senseless process of cluttering up tomorrow's opportunities with leftover problems from today." So if you'd like to make the most out of this day (and every one hereafter), turn your worries over to a Power greater than yourself . . . and spend your valuable time and energy solving the problems you can fix . . . while trusting God to do the rest.

Worry does not empty tomorrow of its sorrow; it empties today of its strength.

Corrie ten Boom

Today is mine. Tomorrow is none of my business. If I peer anxiously into the fog of the future, I will strain my spiritual eyes so that I will not see clearly what is required of me now.

Elisabeth Elliott

The beginning of anxiety is the end of faith, and the beginning of true faith is the end of anxiety.

George Mueller

A PRAYER FOR MOMS

Dear Lord, wherever I find myself, let me celebrate more and worry less. When my faith begins to waver, help me to trust You more. Then, with praise on my lips and the love of Your Son in my heart, let me live courageously, faithfully, prayerfully, and thankfully this day and every day. Amen

What does the Bible say about the need to serve others?

THE QUICK ANSWER

Whether you realize it or not, God has called you to a life of service. Your job is to find a place to serve and to get busy.

A Willingness to Serve

Whoever wants to become great among you must serve the rest of you like a servant.
Matthew 20:26 NCV

Jesus teaches that the most esteemed men and women are not the leaders of society or the captains of industry. To the contrary, Jesus teaches that the greatest among us are those who choose to minister and to serve.

Today, you may feel the temptation to build yourself up in the eyes of your neighbors. Resist that temptation. Instead, serve your neighbors quietly and without fanfare. Find a need and fill it . . . humbly. Lend a helping hand and share a word of kindness . . . anonymously.

Today, take the time to minister to those in need. Then, when you have done your best to serve your neighbors and to serve your God, you can rest comfortably knowing that in the eyes of God you have achieved greatness. And God's eyes, after all, are the only ones that really count.

Christianity, in its purest form, is nothing more than seeing Jesus. Christian service, in its purest form, is nothing more than imitating him who we see. To see his Majesty and to imitate him: that is the sum of Christianity.

Max Lucado

Through our service to others, God wants to influence our world for Him.

Vonette Bright

In the very place where God has put us, whatever its limitations, whatever kind of work it may be, we may indeed serve the Lord Christ.

Elisabeth Elliot

A PRAYER FOR MOMS

Dear Lord, as a mother, I am an example to every member of my family. Give me a servant's heart and make me a faithful steward of my gifts. Let me follow in the footsteps of Your Son Jesus who taught us by example that to be great in Your eyes, Lord, is to serve others humbly, faithfully, and lovingly. Amen

QUESTION 90

What does God's Word say about grace?

THE QUICK ANSWER

God's grace is always available. Jim Cymbala writes, "No one is beyond his grace. No situation, anywhere on earth, is too hard for God." If you sincerely seek God's grace, He will give it freely. So ask, and you will receive.

God's Good News

Thanks be to God for his indescribable gift!
2 Corinthians 9:15 NIV

Christ died on the cross so that we might have eternal life. This gift, freely given from God's only Son, is the priceless possession of everyone who accepts Him as Lord and Savior.

Thankfully, God's grace is not an earthly reward for righteous behavior; it is, instead, a blessed spiritual gift. When we accept Christ into our hearts, we are saved by His grace. The familiar words from the book of Ephesians make God's promise perfectly clear: "For it is by grace you have been saved, through faith—and this not from yourselves, it is the gift of God—not by works, so that no one can boast" (2:8-9 NIV).

God's grace is the ultimate gift, and we owe Him our eternal gratitude. Our Heavenly Father is waiting patiently for each of us to accept His Son and receive His grace. Let us accept that gift today so that we might enjoy God's presence now and throughout all eternity.

Grace is not about finishing last or first; it is about not counting. We receive grace as a gift from God, not as something we toil to earn.

Philip Yancey

God does amazing works through prayers that seek to extend His grace to others.

Shirley Dobson

The grace of God is sufficient for all our needs, for every problem, and for every difficulty, for every broken heart, and for every human sorrow.

Peter Marshall

A PRAYER FOR MOMS

Accepting Your grace can be hard, Lord. Somehow, I feel that I must earn Your love and Your acceptance. Yet, the Bible promises that You love me and save me by Your grace. It is a gift I can only accept and cannot earn. Thank You for Your priceless, everlasting gift. Amen

I have challenges that leave me breathless. What can I do?

THE QUICK ANSWER

Turn to God. The Bible promises that He is sufficient to meet your every need.

He Is Sufficient

And He said to me, "My grace is sufficient for you,
for My strength is made perfect in weakness."
2 Corinthians 12:9 NKJV

Of this you can be certain: God is sufficient to meet your needs. Period.

Do the demands of motherhood seem overwhelming at times? If so, you must learn to rely not only upon your own resources, but also upon the promises of your Father in heaven. God will hold your hand and walk with you and your family if you let Him. So even if your circumstances are difficult, trust the Father.

The Psalmist writes, "Weeping may endure for a night, but joy comes in the morning" (Psalm 30:5 NKJV). But when we are suffering, the morning may seem very far away. It is not. God promises that He is "near to those who have a broken heart" (Psalm 34:18 NKJV). When we are troubled, we must turn to Him, and we must encourage our friends and family members to do likewise.

If you are discouraged by the inevitable demands of life here on earth, be mindful of this fact: the loving heart of God is sufficient to meet any challenge . . . including yours.

Yes, God's grace is always sufficient, and His arms are always open to give it. But, will our arms be open to receive it?

Beth Moore

I grew up learning to be self-reliant, but now, to grow up in Christ, I must unlearn self-reliance and learn self-distrust in light of his all-sufficiency.

Mary Morrison Suggs

God's saints in all ages have realized that God was enough for them. God is enough for time; God is enough for eternity. God is enough!

Hannah Whitall Smith

A PRAYER FOR MOMS

Dear Lord, as I face the challenges of this day, You protect me. I thank You, Father, for Your love and for Your strength. I will lean upon You today and forever. Amen

How does the Bible instruct me to direct my thoughts?

THE QUICK ANSWER

Watch what you think: If your inner voice is, in reality, your inner critic, you need to tone down the criticism now. And while you're at it, train yourself to begin thinking thoughts that are more rational, more accepting, and less judgmental.

The Direction of Your Thoughts

Fix your thoughts on what is true and honorable and right.
Think about things that are pure and lovely and admirable.
Think about things that are excellent and worthy of praise.
Philippians 4:8 NLT

Thoughts are intensely powerful things. Our thoughts have the power to lift us up or drag us down; they have the power to energize us or deplete us, to inspire us to greater accomplishments or to make those accomplishments impossible.

How will you and your family members direct your thoughts today? Will you obey the words of Philippians 4:8 by dwelling upon those things that are honorable, true, and worthy of praise? Or will you allow your thoughts to be hijacked by the negativity that seems to dominate our troubled world?

Are you fearful, angry, bored, or worried? Are you so preoccupied with the concerns of this day that you fail to thank God for the promise of eternity? Are you confused, bitter, or pessimistic? If so, God wants to have a little talk with you.

God intends that you experience joy and abundance, but He will not force His joy upon you; you must claim it for yourself. It's up to you and your loved ones to celebrate the life that God has given you by focusing your minds upon "whatever is commendable." So form the habit of spending more time thinking about your blessings and less time fretting about your hardships. Then, take time to thank the Giver of all things good for gifts that are, in truth, far too numerous to count.

Every major spiritual battle is in the mind.

Charles Stanley

A PRAYER FOR MOMS

Dear Lord, I will focus on Your love, Your power, Your promises, and Your Son. When I am weak, I will turn to You for strength; when I am worried, I will turn to You for comfort; when I am troubled, I will turn to You for patience and perspective. Help me guard my thoughts, Lord, so that I may honor You this day and forever. Amen

I would like to believe that I am protected by God. What does the Bible say about that?

THE QUICK ANSWER

You are protected by God . . . now and always. Earthly security is an illusion. Your only real security comes from the loving heart of God.

The Ultimate Protection

The Lord is my rock, my fortress, and my deliverer, my God, my mountain where I seek refuge. My shield, the horn of my salvation, my stronghold, my refuge, and my Savior.
2 Samuel 22:2-3 HCSB

As a busy woman, you know from firsthand experience that life is not always easy. But as a recipient of God's grace, you also know that you are protected by a loving Heavenly Father.

In times of trouble, God will comfort you; in times of sorrow, He will dry your tears. When you are troubled or weak or sorrowful, God is neither distant nor disinterested. To the contrary, God is always present and always vitally engaged in the events of your life. Reach out to Him, and build your future on the rock that cannot be shaken . . . trust in God and rely upon His provisions. He can provide everything you really need . . . and far, far more.

He goes before us, follows behind us, and hems us safe inside the realm of His protection.

Beth Moore

Prayer is our pathway not only to divine protection, but also to a personal, intimate relationship with God.

Shirley Dobson

The Lord God of heaven and earth, the Almighty Creator of all things, He who holds the universe in His hand as though it were a very little thing, He is your Shepherd, and He has charged Himself with the care and keeping of you, as a shepherd is charged with the care and keeping of his sheep.

Hannah Whitall Smith

A PRAYER FOR MOMS

Lord, You have promised to protect me, and I will trust You. Today, I will live courageously as I place my hopes, my faith, and my life in Your hands. Let my life be a testimony to the transforming power of Your love, Your grace, and Your Son. Amen

What does the Bible say about fearing God?

THE QUICK ANSWER

It's simple: If you have a healthy fear of God, you're wise—if you don't, you're not.

The Right Kind of Fear

The fear of the Lord is the beginning of knowledge,
but fools despise wisdom and discipline.
Proverbs 1:7 NIV

Are you a woman who possesses a healthy, fearful respect for God's power? Hopefully so. After all, God's Word teaches that the fear of the Lord is the beginning of knowledge (Proverbs 1:7).

When we fear the Creator—and when we honor Him by obeying His commandments—we receive God's approval and His blessings. But, when we ignore Him or disobey His commandments, we invite disastrous consequences.

God's hand shapes the universe, and it shapes our lives. God maintains absolute sovereignty over His creation, and His power is beyond comprehension. The fear of the Lord is, indeed, the beginning of knowledge. But thankfully, once we possess a healthy, reverent fear of God, we need never be fearful of anything else.

The remarkable thing about fearing God is that when you fear God, you fear nothing else, whereas if you do not fear God, you fear everything else.

Oswald Chambers

When true believers are awed by the greatness of God and by the privilege of becoming His children, then they become sincerely motivated, effective evangelists.

Bill Hybels

God is so inconceivably good. He's not looking for perfection. He already saw it in Christ. He's looking for affection.

Beth Moore

A PRAYER FOR MOMS

Dear Lord, others have expectations of me, and I have hopes and desires for my life. Lord, bring all other expectations in line with Your plans for me. May my only fear be that of displeasing the One who created me. May I obey Your commandments and seek Your will this day and every day. Amen

Sometimes, I find myself being overly critical of other people, overly critical of my circumstances, or overly critical of myself. What should I do?

THE QUICK ANSWER

Since God's Word instructs you to treat others in the same way you'd like to be treated, you should learn to catch yourself before your "inner critic" becomes fully engaged or enraged.

Beyond Negativity

Don't speak evil against each other, my dear brothers
and sisters. If you criticize each other and condemn each other,
then you are criticizing and condemning God's law.
But you are not a judge who can decide whether the law
is right or wrong. Your job is to obey it.
James 4:11 NLT

From experience, we know that it is easier to criticize than to correct; we understand that it is easier to find faults than solutions; and we realize that excessive criticism is usually destructive, not productive. Yet the urge to criticize others remains a powerful temptation for most of us. Our task, as obedient believers, is to break the twin habits of negative thinking and critical speech.

Negativity is highly contagious: we give it to others who, in turn, give it back to us. This cycle can be broken by positive thoughts, heartfelt prayers, and encouraging words. As thoughtful servants of a loving God, we can use the transforming power of Christ's love to break the chains of negativity. And we should.

I still believe we ought to talk about Jesus. The old country doctor of my boyhood days always began his examination by saying, "Let me see your tongue." That's a good way to check a Christian: the tongue test. Let's hear what he is talking about.

Vance Havner

When you talk, choose the very same words that you would use if Jesus were looking over your shoulder. Because He is.

Marie T. Freeman

A PRAYER FOR MOMS

Help me, Lord, rise above the need to criticize others. May my own shortcomings humble me, and may I always be a source of genuine encouragement to my family and friends. Amen

QUESTION 96

I have big dreams. What should I do about them?

THE QUICK ANSWER

Making your dreams come true requires work. John Maxwell writes "The gap between your vision and your present reality can only be filled through a commitment to maximize your potential." Enough said.

Big Dreams

Live full lives, full in the fullness of God. God can do anything, you know—far more than you could ever imagine or guess or request in your wildest dreams! He does it not by pushing us around but by working within us, his Spirit deeply and gently within us.
Ephesians 3:19-20 MSG

Are you willing to entertain the possibility that God has big plans in store for you and your family? Hopefully so. Yet sometimes, especially if you've recently experienced a life-altering disappointment, you may find it difficult to envision a brighter future for yourself and your family. If so, it's time to reconsider your own capabilities . . . and God's.

Your Heavenly Father created you with unique gifts and untapped talents; your job is to tap them. When you do, you'll begin to feel an increasing sense of confidence in yourself and in your future.

It takes courage to dream big dreams. You will discover that courage when you do three things: accept the past, trust God to handle the future, and make the most of the time He has given you today.

Nothing is too difficult for God, and no dreams are too big for Him—not even yours. So start living—and dreaming—accordingly.

You cannot out-dream God.

John Eldredge

Allow your dreams a place in your prayers and plans. God-given dreams can help you move into the future He is preparing for you.

Barbara Johnson

A PRAYER FOR MOMS

Dear Lord, give me the courage to dream and the faithfulness to trust in Your perfect plan. When I am worried or weary, give me strength for today and hope for tomorrow. Keep me mindful of Your healing power, Your infinite love, and Your eternal salvation. Amen

What does the Bible say about the need to share my personal testimony with family and friends?

THE QUICK ANSWER

If your eternity with God is secure (because you've given your heart to Jesus), you have a profound responsibility to tell as many people as you can about the eternal life that Christ offers to those who believe in Him. And, of course, it's up to you to make sure that your family members know where you stand.

Your Testimony

And I say to you, anyone who acknowledges Me before men,
the Son of Man will also acknowledge him before the angels of God;
but whoever denies Me before men will be denied
before the angels of God.
Luke 12:8-9 HCSB

In his second letter to Timothy, Paul offers a message to believers of every generation when he writes, "God has not given us a spirit of timidity" (1:7 NASB). Paul's meaning is crystal clear: When sharing our testimonies, we, as Christians, must be courageous, forthright, and unashamed.

We live in a world that desperately needs the healing message of Christ Jesus. Every believer, each in his or her own way, bears a personal responsibility for sharing that message. If you are a believer in Christ, you know how He has touched your heart and changed your life. Now it's your turn to share the Good News with others. And remember: today is the perfect time to share your testimony because tomorrow may quite simply be too late.

Claim the joy that is yours. Pray. And know that your joy is used by God to reach others.

Kay Arthur

Faith in small things has repercussions that ripple all the way out. In a huge, dark room a little match can light up the place.

Joni Eareckson Tada

A PRAYER FOR MOMS

Lord, the life that I live and the words that I speak will tell my family and the world how I feel about You. Today and every day, let my testimony be worthy of You. Let my words be sure and true, and let my actions point others to You. Amen

QUESTION 98

What does the Bible say about righteousness?

THE QUICK ANSWER

Because God is just, He rewards righteousness just as surely as He punishes sin. Try as we might, we simply cannot escape the consequences of our actions. How we behave today has a direct impact on the rewards we will receive tomorrow. That's a lesson that we must teach our children by our words and our actions, but not necessarily in that order.

Today's Decisions

The righteous one will live by his faith.
Habakkuk 2:4 HCSB

God has given us a guidebook for righteous living called the Holy Bible. It contains thorough instructions which, if followed, lead to fulfillment, righteousness, and salvation. But, if we choose to ignore God's commandments, the results are as predictable as they are tragic.

The Bible instructs us that a righteous life has many components: faith, honesty, generosity, love, kindness, humility, gratitude, and worship, to name but a few. And, if we seek to follow the steps of our Savior, Jesus Christ, we must, to the best of our abilities, live according to the principles contained in God's Holy Word.

As a loving mother, you are keenly aware that God has entrusted you with a profound responsibility: caring for the needs of your family, including their spiritual needs. To fulfill that responsibility, you must study God's Word and live by it. When you do, your example will be a blessing not only to your loved ones, but also to generations yet unborn.

Righteousness comes only from God.

Kay Arthur

When we do what is right, we have contentment, peace, and happiness.

Beverly LaHaye

Holiness is not an impossibility for any of us.

Elisabeth Elliot

A PRAYER FOR MOMS

Dear Lord, let me obey Your Word, and let me teach my children to do the same. Make me a mother who obeys Your commandments, and let me walk righteously in the footsteps of Your Son, today and every day. Amen

QUESTION 99

What does the Bible have to say about my life?

THE QUICK ANSWER

Every human life (including yours) is a precious gift from God. So celebrate! And while you're at it, praise God for His blessings, and follow in the footsteps of His Son. When you do these things, you'll experience the peace and abundance that only God can give.

Your Wonderful Life

I have set before you life and death, blessings and curses.
Now choose life, so that you and your children may live
and that you may love the LORD your God, listen to his voice,
and hold fast to him.
Deuteronomy 30:19-20 NIV

Each day, as we awaken from sleep and begin the new day, we are confronted with countless opportunities to serve God and to worship Him. When we do, He blesses us. But, if we turn our backs to the Creator, or, if we are simply too busy to acknowledge His greatness, we do ourselves a profound disservice.

As women in a fast-changing world, we face challenges that sometimes leave us feeling overworked, over-committed, and overwhelmed. But God has different plans for us. He intends that we take time each day to slow down long enough to praise Him and glorify His Son. When we do, our spirits are calmed and our lives are enriched, as are the lives of our families and friends.

Each day provides a glorious opportunity to place ourselves in the service of the One who is the Giver of all blessings. May we seek His will, trust His Word, and place Him where He belongs: at the center of our lives.

Life is a glorious opportunity.

Billy Graham

The Christian life is motivated, not by a list of do's and don'ts, but by the gracious outpouring of God's love and blessing.

Anne Graham Lotz

Life is simply hard. That's all there is to it. Thank goodness, the intensity of difficulty rises and falls. Some seasons are far more bearable than others, but none is without challenge.

Beth Moore

A PRAYER FOR MOMS

Lord, You have given me the gift of life. Let me treasure it, and let me use it for Your service and for Your glory. Amen

QUESTION 100

What does the Bible say about God's love?

THE QUICK ANSWER

When all else fails, God's love does not. You can always depend upon God's love . . . and He is always your ultimate protection.

How Much Love?

We know how much God loves us, and we have put our trust in him. God is love, and all who live in love live in God, and God lives in them.

1 John 4:16 NLT

As a mother, you know the profound love that you hold in your heart for your own children. As a child of God, you can only imagine the infinite love that your Heavenly Father holds for you.

God made you in His own image and gave you salvation through the person of His Son Jesus Christ. And now, precisely because you are a wondrous creation treasured by God, a question presents itself: What will you do in response to the Creator's love? Will you ignore it or embrace it? Will you return it or neglect it? That decision, of course, is yours and yours alone.

When you embrace God's love, you are forever changed. When you embrace God's love, you feel differently about yourself, your neighbors, your family, and your world. More importantly, you share God's message—and His love—with others.

Your Heavenly Father—a God of infinite love and mercy—is waiting to embrace you with open arms. Accept His love today and forever.

Jesus loves us with fidelity, purity, constancy, and passion, no matter how imperfect we are.

Stormie Omartian

Nails didn't hold Jesus on the cross. His love for you did.

Anonymous

Being loved by Him whose opinion matters most gives us the security to risk loving, too—even loving ourselves.

Gloria Gaither

A PRAYER FOR MOMS

Thank You, Dear God, for Your love. You are my loving Father—help me to be a loving mother. You are my Creator: I will praise You; I will worship You; and I will love You . . . today, tomorrow, and forever. Amen

Serve him completely and willingly,
because the Lord knows
what is in everyone's mind.
He understands everything you think.
If you go to him for help,
you will get an answer.

—

1 Chronicles 28:9 NCV